B
S

English Men of Letters

EDITED BY JOHN MORLEY

Sterne

by

H. D. TRAILL, B.A., D.C.L.

AUTHOR OF

"COLERIDGE" "SHAFTESBURY" "WILLIAM III."
"LIFE OF SIR JOHN FRANKLIN" ETC.

English Men of Letters

EDITED BY

JOHN MORLEY

HARPER & BROTHERS PUBLISHERS
NEW YORK AND LONDON
1901

U. of Chattanooga

9

5-21- 52 hr

1-23 - 53 cdm

PREFATORY NOTE.

THE materials for a biography of Sterne are by no means abundant. Of the earlier years of his life the only existing record is that preserved in the brief autobiographical memoir which, a few months before his death, he composed, in the usual quaint *staccato* style of his familiar correspondence, for the benefit of his daughter. Of his childhood; of his school-days; of his life at Cambridge, and in his Yorkshire vicarage; of his whole history, in fact, up to the age of forty-six, we know nothing more than he has there jotted down. He attained that age in the year 1759; and at this date begins that series of his *Letters*, from which, for those who have the patience to sort them out of the chronological confusion in which his daughter and editress involved them, there is, no doubt, a good deal to be learnt. These letters, however, which extend down to 1768, the year of the writer's death, contain pretty nearly all the contemporary material that we have to depend on. Freely as Sterne mixed in the best literary society, there is singularly little to be gathered about him, even in the way of chance allusion and anecdote, from the memoirs and *ana* of his time. Of the many friends who would have been competent to write his biography while the facts were yet fresh, but one, John Wilkes, ever entertained—if he did seriously entertain—the idea of performing this pious work; and he, in spite of the entreaties of Sterne's widow

and daughter, then in straitened circumstances, left unre-
deemed his promise to do so.   The brief memoir by Sir
Walter Scott, which is prefixed to many popular editions
of *Tristram Shandy* and the *Sentimental Journey*, sets out
the so-called autobiography in full, but for the rest is mainly critical; Thackeray's well-known lecture-essay is almost
wholly so; and nothing, worthy to be dignified by the
name of a *Life of Sterne*, seems ever to have been published, until the appearance of Mr. Percy Fitzgerald's two
stout volumes, under this title, some eighteen years ago.
Of this work it is hardly too much to say that it contains
(no doubt with the admixture of a good deal of superflu-
ous matter) nearly all the information as to the facts of
Sterne's life that is now ever likely to be recovered.   The
evidence for certain of its statements of fact is not as thoroughly sifted as it might have been; and with some of its
criticism I, at least, am unable to agree.   But no one interested in the subject of this memoir can be insensible of his
obligations to Mr. Fitzgerald for the fruitful diligence with
which he has laboured in a too long neglected field.

H. D. T.

CONTENTS.

STERNE.

CHAPTER I.

(1713–1724.)

TOWARDS the close of the month of November, 1713, one of the last of the English regiments which had been detained in Flanders to supervise the execution of the treaty of Utrecht arrived at Clonmel from Dunkirk. The day after its arrival the regiment was disbanded; and yet a few days later, on the 24th of the month, the wife of one of its subalterns gave birth to a son. The child who thus early displayed the perversity of his humour by so inopportune an appearance was LAURENCE STERNE. "My birthday," he says, in the slipshod, loosely-strung notes by which he has been somewhat grandiloquently said to have "anticipated the labours" of the biographer—"my birthday was ominous to my poor father, who was the day after our arrival, with many other brave officers, broke and sent adrift into the wide world with a wife and two children." Roger Sterne, however, now late ensign of the 34th, or Chudleigh's regiment of foot, was after all in less evil case than were many, probably, of his comrades. He had kins-

1*

men to whom he could look for, at any rate, temporary
assistance, and his mother was a wealthy widow. The
Sternes, originally of a Suffolk stock, had passed from that
county to Nottinghamshire, and thence into Yorkshire, and
were at this time a family of position and substance in the
last-named county. Roger's grandfather had been Archbishop of York, and a man of more note, if only through
the accident of the times upon which he fell, than most of
the incumbents of that see. He had played an exceptionally energetic part even for a Cavalier prelate in the great
political struggle of the seventeenth century, and had suffered with fortitude and dignity in the royal cause. He
had, moreover, a further claim to distinction in having been
treated with common gratitude at the Restoration by the
son of the monarch whom he had served. As Master of
Jesus College, Cambridge, he had "been active in sending
the University plate to his Majesty," and for this offence
he was seized by Cromwell and carried in military custody
to London, whence, after undergoing imprisonment in various gaols, and experiencing other forms of hardship, he
was at length permitted to retire to an obscure retreat in
the country, there to commune with himself until that
tyranny should be overpast. On the return of the exiled
Stuarts Dr. Sterne was made Bishop of Carlisle, and a few
years later was translated to the see of York. He lived
to the age of eighty-six, and so far justified Burnet's accu-
sation against him of "minding chiefly enriching himself,"
that he seems to have divided no fewer than four landed
estates among his children. One of these, Simon Sterne,
a younger son of the Archbishop, himself married an heir-
ess, the daughter of Sir Roger Jaques of Elvington; and
Roger, the father of Laurence Sterne, was the seventh and
youngest of the issue of this marriage. At the time when

the double misfortune above recorded befell him at the
hands of Lucina and the War Office, his father had been
some years dead; but Simon Sterne's widow was still mistress of the property which she had brought with her at
her marriage, and to Elvington, accordingly, "as soon,"
writes Sterne, "as I was able to be carried," the compul-
sorily retired ensign betook himself with his wife and his
two children. He was not, however, compelled to remain
long dependent on his mother. The ways of the military
authorities were as inscrutable to the army of that day as
they are in our day to our own. Before a year had passed
the regiment was ordered to be re-established, and "our
household decamped with bag and baggage for Dublin."
This was in the autumn of 1714, and from that time onward, for some eleven years, the movements and fortunes
of the Sterne family, as detailed in the narrative of its
most famous member, form a history in which the ludicrous struggles strangely with the pathetic.

A husband, condemned to be the Ulysses-like plaything
of adverse gods at the War Office; an indefatigably pro-
lific wife; a succession of weak and ailing children; misfortune in the seasons of journeying; misfortune in the
moods of the weather by sea and land—under all this
combination of hostile chances and conditions was the
struggle to be carried on. The little household was perpetually "on the move"—a little household which was
always becoming and never remaining bigger—continually increased by births, only to be again reduced by deaths
—until the contest between the deadly hardships of travel and the fatal fecundity of Mrs. Sterne was brought by
events to a natural close. Almost might the unfortunate
lady have exclaimed, *Quæ regio in terris nostri non plena
laboris?* She passes from Ireland to England, and from

England to Ireland, from inland garrison to sea-port town
and back again, incessantly bearing and incessantly burying children—until even her son in his narrative begins to
speak of losing one infant at this place, and "leaving another behind" on that journey, almost as if they were so
many overlooked or misdirected articles of luggage. The
tragic side of the history, however, overshadows the grotesque. When we think how hard a business was travel
even under the most favourable conditions in those days,
and how serious even in our own times, when travel is
easy, are the discomforts of the women and children of a
regiment on the march—we may well pity these unrest-
ing followers of the drum. As to Mrs. Sterne herself, she
seems to have been a woman of a pretty tough fibre, and
she came moreover of a campaigning stock. Her father
was a "noted suttler" of the name of Nuttle, and her first
husband—for she was a widow when Roger Sterne married
her—had been a soldier also. She had, therefore, served
some years' apprenticeship to the military life before these
wanderings began; and she herself was destined to live
to a good old age. But somehow or other she failed to
endow her offspring with her own robust constitution and
powers of endurance. "My father's children were," as
Laurence Sterne grimly puts it, "not made to last long;"
but one cannot help suspecting that it was the hardships
of those early years which carried them off in their infancy with such painful regularity and despatch, and that it
was to the same cause that their surviving brother owed
the beginnings of that fatal malady by which his own life
was cut short.

The diary of their travels—for the early part of Sterne's
memoirs amounts to scarcely more—is the more effective
for its very brevity and abruptness. Save for one interval

of somewhat longer sojourn than usual at Dublin, the reader has throughout it all the feeling of the traveller who
never finds time to unpack his portmanteau. On the re-
enrolment of the regiment in 1714, " our household," says
the narrative, " decamped from York with bag and baggage for Dublin. Within a month my father left us, being ordered to Exeter; where, in a sad winter, my mother
and her two children followed him, travelling from Liver-
pool, by land, to Plymouth." At Plymouth Mrs. Sterne
gave birth to a son, christened Joram; and, " in twelve
months' time we were all sent back to Dublin. My mother," with her three children, " took ship at Bristol for Ireland, and had a narrow escape from being cast away by a
leak springing up in the vessel. At length, after many
perils and struggles, we got to Dublin." Here intervenes
the short breathing-space, of which mention has been made
—an interval employed by Roger Sterne in " spending a
great deal of money" on a " large house," which he hired
and furnished; and then " in the year one thousand seven
hundred and nineteen, all unhinged again." The regiment
had been ordered off to the Isle of Wight, thence to em-
bark for Spain, on " the Vigo Expedition," and " we," who
accompanied it, " were driven into Milford Haven, but afterwards landed at Bristol, and thence by land to Plymouth
again, and to the Isle of Wight;" losing on this expedition " poor Joram, a pretty boy, who died of the small-
pox." In the Isle of Wight, Mrs. Sterne and her family
remained till the Vigo Expedition returned home; and
during her stay there " poor Joram's loss was supplied by
the birth of a girl, Anne," a " pretty blossom," but destined
to fall " at the age of three years." On the return of the
regiment to Wicklow, Roger Sterne again sent to collect
his family around him. " We embarked for Dublin, and

had all been cast away by a most violent storm; but,
through the intercession of my mother, the captain was
prevailed upon to turn back into Wales, where we stayed
a month, and at length got into Dublin, and travelled by
land to Wicklow, where my father had, for some weeks,
given us over for lost." Here a year passed, and another
child, Devijeher—so called after the colonel of the regiment—was born. "From thence we decamped to stay
half a year with Mr. Fetherston, a clergyman, about seven
miles from Wicklow, who, being a relative of my mother's,
invited us to his parsonage at Animo.[1] From thence,
again, "we followed the regiment to Dublin," where again
"we lay in the barracks a year." In 1722 the regiment
was ordered to Carrickfergus. "We all decamped, but
got no further than Drogheda; thence ordered to Mullin-
gar, forty miles west, where, by Providence, we stumbled
upon a kind relation, a collateral descendant from Archbishop Sterne, who took us all to his castle, and kindly entertained us for a year." Thence, by "a most rueful journey," to Carrickfergus, where "we arrived in six or seven

---

[1] "It was in this parish," says Sterne, "that I had that wonderful
escape in falling through a mill race while the mill was going, and
being taken up unhurt; the story is incredible, but known to all that
part of Ireland, where hundreds of the common people flocked to see
me." More incredible still does it seem that Thoresby should relate
the occurrence of an accident of precisely the same kind to Sterne's
great-grandfather, the Archbishop. "Playing near a mill, he fell within a claw; there was but one board or bucket wanting in the whole
wheel, but a gracious Providence so ordered it that the void place
came down at that moment, else he had been crushed to death; but
was reserved to be a grand benefactor afterwards." (Thoresby, ii. 15.)
But what will probably strike the reader as more extraordinary even
than this coincidence is that Sterne should have been either unaware
of it, or should have omitted mention of it in the above passage.

days." Here, at the age of three, little Devijeher obtained a happy release from his name; and "another child, Susan, was sent to fill his place, who also left us behind in this weary journey." In the "autumn of this year, or the spring of the next"—Sterne's memory failing in exactitude at the very point where we should have expected it to be most precise—"my father obtained permission of his colonel to fix me at school;" and henceforth the boy's share in the family wanderings was at an end. But his father had yet to be ordered from Carrickfergus to Londonderry, where at last a permanent child, Catherine, was born; and thence to Gibraltar, to take part in the Defence of that famous Rock, where the much-enduring campaigner was run through the body in a duel, "about a goose" (a thoroughly Shandian catastrophe); and thence to Jamaica, where, "with a constitution impaired" by the sword-thrust earned in his anserine quarrel, he was defeated in a more deadly duel with the "country fever," and died. "His malady," writes his son, with a touch of feeling struggling through his dislocated grammar, "took away his senses first, and made a child of him; and then in a month or two walking about continually without complaining, till the moment he sat down in an arm-chair and breathed his last."

There is, as has been observed, a certain mixture of the comic and the pathetic in the life-history of this obscure father of a famous son. His life was clearly not a fortunate one, so far as external circumstances go; but its misfortunes had no sort of consoling dignity about them Roger Sterne's lot in the world was not so much an unhappy as an uncomfortable one; and discomfort earns little sympathy, and absolutely no admiration, for its sufferers. He somehow reminds us of one of those Irish heroes

—good-natured, peppery, debt-loaded, light-hearted, shift-
less — whose fortunes we follow with mirthful and half-
contemptuous sympathy in the pages of Thackeray. He
was obviously a typical specimen of that class of men who
are destitute alike of the virtues and failings of the "respectable" and successful; whom many people love and
no one respects; whom everybody pities in their struggles
and difficulties, but whom few pity without a smile.

It is evident, however, that he succeeded in winning the
affection of one who had not too much affection of the
deeper kind to spare for any one. The figure of Roger
Sterne alone stands out with any clearness by the side of
the ceaselessly flitting mother and phantasmal children of
Laurence Sterne's Memoir; and it is touched in with strokes
so vivid and characteristic that critics have been tempted
to find in it the original of the most famous portrait in
the Shandy gallery. "My father," says Sterne, "was a
little, smart man, active to the last degree in all exercises,
most patient of fatigue and disappointments, of which it
pleased God to give him full measure. He was, in his
temper, somewhat rapid and hasty, but of a kindly, sweet
disposition, void of all design, and so innocent in his own
intentions, that he suspected no one; so that you might
have cheated him ten times a day, if nine had not been
sufficient for your purpose." This is a captivating little
picture; and it no doubt presents traits which may have
impressed themselves early and deeply on the imagination
which was afterwards to give birth to "My Uncle Toby."
The simplicity of nature and the "kindly, sweet disposition" are common to both the ensign of real life and to
the immortal Captain Shandy of fiction; but the criticism
which professes to find traces of Roger Sterne's "rapid and
hasty temper" in my Uncle Toby is compelled to strain

itself considerably. And, on the whole, there seems no reason to believe that Sterne borrowed more from the character of his father than any writer must necessarily, and perhaps unconsciously, borrow from his observation of the moral and mental qualities of those with whom he has come into most frequent contact.

That Laurence Sterne passed the first eleven years of his life with such an exemplar of these simple virtues of kindliness, guilelessness, and courage ever before him, is perhaps the best that can be said for the lot in which his early days were cast. In almost all other respects there could hardly have been—for a quick-witted, precocious, imitative boy — a worse bringing-up. No one, I should imagine, ever more needed discipline in his youth than Sterne; and the camp is a place of discipline for the soldier only. To all others whom necessity attaches to it, and to the young especially, it is rather a school of license and irregularity. It is fair to remember these disadvantages of Sterne's early training, in judging of the many defects as a man, and laxities as a writer, which marked his later life; though, on the other hand, there is no denying the reality and value of some of the countervailing advantages which came to him from his boyish surroundings. The conception of my Uncle Toby need not have been taken whole from Roger Sterne, or from any one actual captain of a marching regiment; but the constant sight of, and converse with, many captains and many corporals may undoubtedly have contributed much to the vigour and vitality of Toby Shandy and Corporal Trim. So far as the externals of portraiture were concerned, there can be no doubt that his art benefited much from his early military life. His soldiers have the true stamp of the soldier about them in air and language; and when his captain and

corporal fight their Flemish battles over again we are thoroughly conscious that we are listening, under the dramatic
form, to one who must himself have heard many a chapter
of the same splendid story from the lips of the very men
who had helped to break the pride of the Grand Monarque
under Marlborough and Eugene.

CHAPTER II.

IT was not—as we have seen from the Memoir—till the autumn of 1723, "or the spring of the following year," that Roger Sterne obtained leave of his colonel to "fix" his son at school; and this would bring Laurence to the tolerably advanced age of ten before beginning his education in any systematic way. He records, under date of 1721, that "in this year I learned to write, &c.;" but it is not probable that the "&c."—that indolent symbol of which Sterne makes such irritating use in all his familiar writing—covers, in this case, any wide extent of educational advance. The boy, most likely, could just read and write, and no more, at the time when he was fixed at school, "near Halifax, with an able master:" a judicious selection, no doubt, both of place as well as teacher. Mr. Fitzgerald, to whose researches we owe as much light as is ever likely to be thrown upon this obscure and probably not very interesting period of Sterne's life, has pointed out that Richard Sterne, eldest son of the late Simon Sterne, and uncle, therefore, of Laurence, was one of the governors of Halifax Grammar School, and that he may have used his interest to obtain his nephew's admission to the foundation as the grandson of a Halifax man, and so, constructively, a child of the parish. But, be this as it

may, it is more than probable that from the time when
he was sent to Halifax School the whole care and cost of
the boy's education was borne by his Yorkshire relatives.
The Memoir says that, "by God's care of me, my cousin
Sterne, of Elvington, became a father to me, and sent me
to the University, &c., &c. ;" and it is to be inferred from
this that the benevolent guardianship of Sterne's uncle
Richard (who died in 1732, the year before Laurence was
admitted of Jesus College, Cambridge) must have been
taken up by his son. Of his school course — though it
lasted for over seven years—the autobiographer has little
to say ; nothing, indeed, except that he "cannot omit mentioning" that anecdote with which everybody, I suppose,
who has ever come across the briefest notice of Sterne's
life is familiar. The schoolmaster "had the ceiling of
the schoolroom new-whitewashed, and the ladder remained there. I, one unlucky day, mounted it, and wrote with
a brush, in large capital letters, LAU. STERNE, for which
the usher severely whipped me. My master was very
much hurt at this, and said before me that never should
that name be effaced, for I was a boy of genius, and he
was sure I should come to preferment. This expression
made me forget the blows I had received." It is hardly
to be supposed, of course, that this story is pure romance ;
but it is difficult, on the other hand, to believe that the incident has been related by Sterne exactly as it happened.
That the recorded prediction may have been made in jest
—or even in earnest (for penetrating teachers have these
prophetic moments sometimes) — is, of course, possible ;
but that Sterne's master was "very much hurt" at the
boy's having been justly punished for an act of wanton
mischief, or that he recognized it as the natural privilege
of nascent genius to deface newly-whitewashed ceilings,

must have been a delusion of the humourist's later years.
The extreme fatuity which it would compel us to attribute
to the schoolmaster seems inconsistent with the power of
detecting intellectual capacity in any one else. On the
whole, one inclines to suspect that the remark belonged to
that order of half-sardonic, half-kindly jest which a certain
sort of pedagogue sometimes throws off, for the consolation of a recently-caned boy; and that Sterne's vanity,
either then or afterwards (for it remained juvenile all his
life), translated it into a serious prophecy. In itself, however, the urchin's freak was only too unhappily characteristic of the man. The trick of befouling what was clean
(and because it was clean) clung to him most tenaciously
all his days; and many a fair white surface—of humour,
of fancy, or of sentiment—was to be disfigured by him
in after-years with stains and splotches in which we can
all too plainly decipher the literary signature of Laurence
Sterne.

At Halifax School the boy, as has been said, remained
for about eight years; that is, until he was nearly nineteen,
and for some months after his father's death at Port An-
tonio, which occurred in March, 1731. "In the year '32,"
says the Memoir, "my cousin sent me to the University,
where I stayed some time." In the course of his first year
he read for and obtained a sizarship, to which the college
records show that he was duly admitted on the 6th of July,
1733. The selection of Jesus College was a natural one:
Sterne's great-grandfather, the afterwards Archbishop, had
been its Master, and had founded scholarships there, to one
of which the young sizar was, a year after his admission,
elected. No inference can, of course, be drawn from this
as to Sterne's proficiency, or even industry, in his academical studies: it is scarcely more than a testimony to the

fact of decent and regular behaviour. He was *bene natus*, in the sense of being related to the right man, the founder; and in those days he need be only very *modicè doctus* indeed in order to qualify himself for admission to the enjoyment of his kinsman's benefactions. Still he must have been orderly and well-conducted in his ways; and this he would also seem to have been, from the fact of his having passed through his University course without any apparent break or hitch, and having been admitted to his Bachelor's degree after no more than the normal period of residence. The only remark which, in the Memoir, he vouchsafes to bestow upon his academical career is, that " 'twas there that I commenced a friendship with Mr. H——, which has been lasting on both sides;" and it may, perhaps, be said that this *was*, from one point of view, the most important event of his Cambridge life. For Mr. H—— was John Hall, afterwards John Hall Stevenson, the " Eugenius " of *Tristram Shandy*, the master of Skelton Castle, at which Sterne was, throughout life, to be a frequent and most familiar visitor; and, unfortunately, also a person whose later reputation, both as a man and a writer, became such as seriously to compromise the not very robust respectability of his clerical comrade. Sterne and Hall were distant cousins, and it may have been the tie of consanguinity which first drew them together. But there was evidently a thorough congeniality of the most unlucky sort between them; and from their first meeting, as undergraduates at Jesus, until the premature death of the elder, they continued to supply each other's minds with precisely that sort of occupation and stimulus of which each by the grace of nature stood least in need. That their close intimacy was ill-calculated to raise Sterne's reputation in later years may be inferred from the fact that Hall Stevenson afterwards

obtained literary notoriety by the publication of *Crazy
Tales*, a collection of comic but extremely broad ballads,
in which his clerical friend was quite unjustly suspected of
having had a hand.   Mr. Hall was also reported, whether
truly or falsely, to have been a member of Wilkes's famous
confraternity of Medmenham Abbey; and from this it was
an easy step for gossip to advance to the assertion that the
Rev. Mr. Sterne had himself been admitted to that unholy
order.

Among acquaintances which the young sizar of Jesus
might have more profitably made at Cambridge, but did
not, was that of a student destined, like himself, to leave
behind him a name famous in English letters.   Gray, born
three years later than Sterne, had entered a year after him
at Cambridge as a pensioner of Peterhouse, and the two
students went through their terms together, though the
poet at the time took no degree.   There was probably little enough in common between the shy, fastidious, slightly
effeminate pensioner of Peterhouse, and a scholar of Jesus,
whose chief friend and comrade was a man like Hall; and
no close intimacy between the two men, if they had come
across each other, would have been very likely to arise.
But it does not appear that they could have ever met or
heard of each other, for Gray writes of Sterne, after *Tristram Shandy* had made him famous, in terms which clearly show that he did not recall his fellow-undergraduate.

In January, 1736, Sterne took his B.A. degree, and quitted Cambridge for York, where another of his father's
brothers now makes his appearance as his patron.   Dr.
Jacques Sterne was the second son of Simon Sterne, of
Elvington, and a man apparently of more marked and vigorous character than any of his brothers.   What induced
him now to take notice of the nephew, whom in boyhood

and early youth he had left to the unshared guardianship
of his brother, and brother's son, does not appear; but the
personal history of this energetic pluralist—Prebendary of
Durham, Archdeacon of Cleveland, Canon Residentiary,
Precentor, Prebendary, and Archdeacon of York, Rector of
Rise, and Rector of Hornsey-cum-Riston—suggests the sur-
mise that he detected qualities in the young Cambridge
graduate which would make him useful. For Dr. Sterne
was a typical specimen of the Churchman-politician, in
days when both components of the compound word
meant a good deal more than they do now. The Archdeacon was a devoted Whig, a Hanoverian to the back-
bone; and he held it his duty to support the Protestant
succession, not only by the spiritual but by the secular arm.
He was a great electioneerer, as befitted times when the
claims of two rival dynasties virtually met upon the hust-
ings, and he took a prominent part in the great Yorkshire
contest of the year 1734. His most vigorous display of
energy, however, was made, as was natural, in "the '45."
The Whig Archdeacon, not then Archdeacon of the East
Riding, nor as yet quite buried under the mass of preferments which he afterwards accumulated, seems to have
thought that this indeed was the crisis of his fortunes, and
that, unless he was prepared to die a mere prebendary,
canon, and rector of one or two benefices, now was the
time to strike a blow for his advancement in the Church.
His bustling activity at this trying time was indeed por-
tentous, and at last took the form of arresting the unfortunate Dr. Burton (the original of Dr. Slop), on suspicion
of holding communication with the invading army of the
Pretender, then on its march southward from Edinburgh.
The suspect, who was wholly innocent, was taken to London and kept in custody for nearly a year before being

discharged, after which, by way of a slight redress, a letter of reprimand for his *trop de zèle* was sent by direction of Lord Carteret to the militant dignitary. But the desired end was nevertheless attained, and Dr. Sterne succeeded in crowning the edifice of his ecclesiastical honours.[1]

There can be little doubt that patronage extended by such an uncle to such a nephew received its full equivalent in some way or other, and indeed the Memoir gives us a clue to the mode in which payment was made. "My uncle," writes Sterne, describing their subsequent rupture, "quarrelled with me because I would not write paragraphs in the newspapers; though he was a party-man, I was not, and detested such dirty work, thinking it beneath me. From that time he became my bitterest enemy." The date of this quarrel cannot be precisely fixed; but we gather from an autograph letter (now in the British Museum) from Sterne to Archdeacon Blackburne that by the year 1750 the two men had for some time ceased to be on friendly terms. Probably, however, the breach occurred subsequently to the rebellion of '45, and it may be that it arose out of the excess of partisan zeal which Dr. Sterne developed in that year, and which his nephew very likely

---

[1] A once-familiar piece of humorous verse describes the upset of a coach containing a clerical pluralist:

> "When struggling on the ground was seen
> A Rector, Vicar, Canon, Dean;
> You might have thought the coach was full,
> But no! 'twas only Dr. Bull."

Dr. Jacques Sterne, however, might have been thrown out of one of the more capacious vehicles of the London General Omnibus Company, with almost the same misleading effect upon those who only *heard* of the mishap.

2

did not, in his opinion, sufficiently share. But this is
quite consistent with the younger man's having up to that
time assisted the elder in his party polemics. He certainly
speaks in his "Letters" of his having "employed his brains
for an ungrateful person," and the remark is made in a
way and in a connexion which seems to imply that the
services rendered to his uncle were mainly *literary*. If so,
his declaration that he "would not write paragraphs in the
newspapers" can only mean that he would not go on writing them. Be this as it may, however, it is certain that
the Archdeacon for some time found his account in main-
taining friendly relations with his nephew, and that during
that period he undoubtedly did a good deal for his advancement. Sterne was ordained deacon by the Bishop of
Lincoln in March, 1736, only three months after taking his
B.A. degree, and took priest's orders in August, 1738, where-
upon his uncle immediately obtained for him the living of
Sutton-on-the-Forest, into which he was inducted a few
days afterwards. Other preferments followed, to be noted
hereafter; and it must be admitted that until the quarrel
occurred about the "party paragraphs" the Archdeacon
did his duty by his nephew after the peculiar fashion of
that time. When that quarrel came, however, it seems to
have snapped more ties than one, for in the Memoir Sterne
speaks of his youngest sister Catherine as "still living, but
most unhappily estranged from me by my uncle's wicked-
ness and her own folly." Of his elder sister Mary, who
was born at Lille a year before himself, he records that
"she married one Weemans in Dublin, who used her most
unmercifully, spent his substance, became a bankrupt, and
left my poor sister to shift for herself, which she was able
to do but for a few months, for she went to a friend's
house in the country and died of a broken heart." Truly

an unlucky family.[1]   Only three to survive the hardships
among which the years of their infancy were passed, and
this to be the history of two out of the three survivors!

[1] The mother, Mrs. Sterne, makes her appearance once more for a
moment in or about the year 1758.   Horace Walpole, and after him
Byron, accused Sterne of having "preferred whining over a dead ass
to relieving a living mother," and the former went so far as to declare " on indubitable authority" that Mrs. Sterne, "who kept a school
(in Ireland), having run in debt on account of an extravagant daughter, would have rotted in a gaol if the parents of her scholars had not
raised a subscription for her."   Even "the indubitable authority,"
however, does not positively assert—whatever may be meant to be
insinuated—that Sterne himself did nothing to assist his mother,
and Mr. Fitzgerald justly points out that to pay the *whole* debts of
a bankrupt school might well have been beyond a Yorkshire clergyman's means.   Anyhow there is evidence that Sterne at a later date
than this was actively concerning himself about his mother's inter-
ests.   She afterwards came to York, whither he went to meet her;
and he then writes to a friend: "I trust my poor mother's affair is
by this time ended to *our* comfort and hers."

CHAPTER III.

LIFE AT SUTTON.——MARRIAGE.——THE PARISH PRIEST.

(1738–1759.)

GREAT writers who spring late and suddenly from obscurity into fame and yet die early, must always form more or less perplexing subjects of literary biography. The processes of their intellectual and artistic growth lie hidden in nameless years; their genius is not revealed to the world until it has reached its full maturity, and many aspects of it, which, perhaps, would have easily explained themselves if the gradual development had gone on before men's eyes, remain often unexplained to the last. By few, if any, of the more celebrated English men of letters is this observation so forcibly illustrated as it is in the case of Sterne : the obscure period of his life so greatly exceeded in duration the brief season of his fame, and its obscurity was so exceptionally profound. He was forty - seven years of age when, at a bound, he achieved celebrity ; he was not five-and-fifty when he died. And though it might be too much to say that the artist sprang, like the reputation, full-grown into being, it is nevertheless true that there are no marks of positive immaturity to be detected even in the earliest public displays of his art. His work grows, indeed, most marvellously in vividness and symmetry as he proceeds, but there are no visible signs of growth in the workman's skill.

Even when the highest point of finish is attained we cannot say that the hand is any more cunning than it was from the first. As well might we say that the last light touches of the sculptor's chisel upon the perfected statue are more skilful than its first vigorous strokes upon the shapeless block.

It is certain, however, that Sterne must have been storing up his material of observation, secreting his reflections on life and character, and consciously or unconsciously maturing his powers of expression, during the whole of those silent twenty years which have now to be passed under brief review. With one exception, to be noted presently, the only known writings of his which belong to this period are sermons, and these — a mere "scratch" collection of pulpit discourses, which, as soon as he had gained the public ear, he hastened in characteristic fashion to rummage from his desk and carry to the book-market—throw no light upon the problem before us. There are sermons of Sterne which alike in manner and matter disclose the author of *Tristram Shandy;* but they are not among those which he preached or wrote before that work was given to the world. They are not its ancestors but its descendants. They belong to the post-Shandian period, and are in obvious imitation of the Shandian style; while in none of the earlier ones—not even in that famous homily on a Good Conscience, which did not succeed till Corporal Trim preached it before the brothers Shandy and Dr. Slop— can we trace either the trick of style or the turn of thought that give piquancy to the novel. Yet the peculiar qualities of mind, and the special faculty of workmanship of which this turn of thought and trick of style were the product, must of course have been potentially present from the beginning. Men do not blossom forth as wits, hu-

mourists, masterly delineators of character, and skilful performers on a highly-strung and carefully-tuned sentimental
instrument all at once, after entering their "forties;" and
the only wonder is that a possessor of these powers—some
of them of the kind which, as a rule, and in most men,
seeks almost as irresistibly for exercise as even the poetic
instinct itself—should have been held so long unemployed.

There is, however, one very common stimulus to literary
exertions which in Sterne's case was undoubtedly wanting
—a superabundance of unoccupied time. We have little
reason, it is true, to suppose that this light-minded and
valetudinarian Yorkshire parson was at any period of his
life an industrious "parish priest;" but it is probable,
nevertheless, that time never hung very heavily upon his
hands. In addition to the favourite amusements which he
enumerates in the Memoir, he was all his days addicted to
one which is, perhaps, the most absorbing of all—flirtation.
Philandering, and especially philandering of the Platonic
and ultra-sentimental order, is almost the one human pastime of which its votaries never seem to tire; and its constant ministrations to human vanity may serve, perhaps,
to account for their unwearied absorption in its pursuit.
Sterne's first love affair—an affair of which, unfortunately,
the consequences were more lasting than the passion—took
place immediately upon his leaving Cambridge. To relate
it as he relates it to his daughter: "At York I became acquainted with your mother, and courted her for two years.
She owned she liked me, but thought herself not rich
enough or me too poor to be joined together. She went
to her sister's in S[taffordshire], and I wrote to her often.
I believe then she was partly determined to have me, but
would not say so. At her return she fell into a consumption, and one evening that I was sitting by her, with

an almost broken heart to see her so ill, she said: 'My
dear Laury, I never can be yours, for I verily believe I
have not long to live! but I have left you every shil-
ling of my fortune.' Upon that she showed me her will.
This generosity overpowered me. It pleased God that
she recovered, and we were married in 1741." The
name of this lady was Elizabeth Lumley, and it was to
her that Sterne addressed those earliest letters which
his daughter included in the collection published by her
some eight years after her father's death. They were
added, the preface tells us, "in justice to Mr. Sterne's
delicate feelings;" and in our modern usage of the word
"delicate," as equivalent to infirm of health and probably
short of life, they no doubt do full justice to the passion
which they are supposed to express. It would be unfair,
of course, to judge any love-letters of that period by the
standard of sincerity applied in our own less artificial age.
All such compositions seem frigid and formal enough to
us of to-day; yet in most cases of genuine attachment we
usually find at least a sentence here and there in which the
natural accents of the heart make themselves heard above
the affected modulations of the style. But the letters of
Sterne's courtship maintain the pseudo-poetic, shepherd-
and-shepherdess strain throughout; or, if the lover ever
abandons it, it is only to make somewhat maudlin record
of those "tears" which flowed a little too easily at all
times throughout his life. These letters, however, have a
certain critical interest in their bearing upon those sensibilities which Sterne afterwards learned to cultivate in a
forcing-frame, with a view to the application of their produce to the purposes of an art of pathetic writing which
simulates nature with such admirable fidelity at its best,
and descends to such singular bathos at its worst.

The marriage preluded by this courtship did not take
place till Sterne had already been three years Vicar of Sutton-on-the-Forest, the benefice which had been procured
for him by his uncle the Archdeacon; through whose interest also he was appointed successively to two prebends
—preferments which were less valuable to him for their
emolument than for the ecclesiastical status which they
conferred upon him; for the excuse which they gave him
for periodical visits to the cathedral city to fulfil the residential conditions of his offices, and for the opportunity
thus afforded him of mixing in and studying the society
of the Close.   Upon his union with Miss Lumley, and, in
a somewhat curious fashion, by her means, he obtained in
addition the living of Stillington.   "A friend of hers in
the South had promised her that if she married a clergyman in Yorkshire, when the living became vacant he would
make her a compliment of it;" and made accordingly this
singular "compliment" was.   At Sutton Sterne remained
nearly twenty years, doing duty at both places, during
which time "books, painting, fiddling, and shooting were,"
he says, "my chief amusements."   With what success he
shot, and with what skill he fiddled, we know not.   His
writings contain not a few musical metaphors and allusions to music, which seem to indicate a competent acquaintance with its technicalities; but the specimen of
his powers as an artist, which Mr. Fitzgerald has repro-
duced from his illustrations of a volume of poems by Mr.
Woodhull, does not dispose one to rate highly his proficiency in this accomplishment.   We may expect that,
after all, it was the first-mentioned of his amusements in
which he took the greatest delight, and that neither the
brush, the bow, nor the fowling-piece was nearly so often
in his hand as the book.   Within a few miles of Sutton,

at Skelton Castle, an almost unique Roman stronghold,
since modernized by Gothic hands, dwelt his college-friend
John Hall Stevenson, whose well-stocked library contained
a choice but heterogeneous collection of books—old French
"ana," and the learning of mediæval doctors—books in-
tentionally and books unintentionally comic, the former of
which Sterne read with an only too retentive a memory for
their jests, and the latter with an acutely humorous appreciation of their solemn trifling.   Later on it will be time to
note the extent to which he utilized these results of his
widely discursive reading, and to examine the legitimacy of
the mode in which he used them : here it is enough to
say generally that the materials for many a burlesque chapter of *Tristram Shandy* must have been unconsciously
storing themselves in his mind in many an amused hour
passed by Sterne in the library of Skelton Castle.

But before finally quitting this part of my subject it
may be as well, perhaps, to deal somewhat at length with a
matter which will doubtless have to be many times inci-
dentally referred to in the course of this study, but which
I now hope to relieve myself from the necessity of doing
more than touch upon hereafter.   I refer of course to
Sterne's perpetually recurring flirtations.   This is a matter almost as impossible to omit from any biography of
Sterne as it would be to omit it from any biography of
Goethe.   The English humourist did not, it is true, engage
in the pastime in the serious, not to say scientific, spirit of
the German philosopher-poet ; it was not deliberately made
by the former as by the latter to contribute to his artistic
development ; but it is nevertheless hardly open to doubt
that Sterne's philandering propensities did exercise an influence upon his literary character and work in more ways
than one.   That his marriage was an ill-assorted and un-

happy union was hardly so much the cause of his incon-
stancy as its effect. It may well be, of course, that the
"dear L.," whose moral and mental graces her lover had
celebrated in such superfine, sentimental fashion, was a
commonplace person enough. That she was really a woman of the exquisite stolidity of Mrs. Shandy, and that her
exasperating feats as an *assentatrix* did, as has been suggested, supply the model for the irresistibly ludicrous colloquies between the philosopher and his wife, there is no
sufficient warrant for believing. But it is quite possible
that the daily companion of one of the most indefatigable
jesters that ever lived may have been unable to see a joke;
that she regarded her husband's wilder drolleries as mere
horse-collar grimacing, and that the point of his subtler
humour escaped her altogether. But even if it were so, it
is, to say the least of it, doubtful whether Sterne suffered
at all on this ground from the wounded feelings of the
mari incompris, while it is next to certain that it does not
need the sting of any such disappointment to account for
his alienation. He must have had plenty of time and opportunity to discover Miss Lumley's intellectual limitations
during the two years of his courtship; and it is not likely
that, even if they were as well marked as Mrs. Shandy's
own, they would have done much of themselves to estrange
the couple. Sympathy is not the necessity to the humourist which the poet finds, or imagines, it to be to himself:
the humourist, indeed, will sometimes contrive to extract
from the very absence of sympathy in those about him a
keener relish for his reflections. With sentiment, indeed,
and still more with sentimentalism, the case would of course
be different; but as for Mr. Sterne's demands for sympathy in that department of his life and art, one may say
without the least hesitation that they would have been be-

yond the power of any one woman, however distinguished
a disciple of the "Laura Matilda" school, to satisfy. "I
must ever," he frankly says in one of the "Yorick to Eliza"
letters, "I must ever have some Dulcinea in my head: it
harmonizes the soul;" and he might have added that he
found it impossible to sustain the harmony without frequently changing the Dulcinea. One may suspect that
Mrs. Sterne soon had cause for jealousy, and it is at least
certain that several years before Sterne's emergence into
notoriety their estrangement was complete. One daughter
was born to them in 1745, but lived scarcely more than
long enough to be rescued from the *limbus infantium* by
the prompt rites of the Church. The child was christened
Lydia, and died on the following day. Its place was filled
in 1747 by a second daughter, also christened Lydia, who
lived to become the wife of M. de Medalle, and the not
very judicious editress of the posthumous "Letters." For
her as she grew up Sterne conceived a genuine and truly
fatherly affection, and it is in writing to her and of her
that we see him at his best; or rather one might say it is
almost only then that we can distinguish the true notes of
the heart through that habitual falsetto of sentimentalism
which distinguishes most of Sterne's communications with
the other sex. There was no subsequent issue of the marriage, and, from one of the letters most indiscreetly included in Madame de Medalle's collection, it is to be as-
certained that some four years or so after Lydia's birth the
relations between Sterne and Mrs. Sterne ceased to be conjugal, and never again resumed that character.

It is, however, probable, upon the husband's own con-
fessions, that he had given his wife earlier cause for jealousy, and certainly from the time when he begins to reveal himself in correspondence there seems to be hardly

a moment when some such cause was not in existence —in the person of this, that, or the other lackadaisical damsel or coquettish matron. From Miss Fourmantelle, the "dear, dear Kitty," to whom Sterne was making violent love in 1759, the year of the York publication of *Tristram Shandy*, down to Mrs. Draper, the heroine of the famous "Yorick to Eliza" letters, the list of ladies who seem to have kindled flames in that susceptible breast is almost as long and more real than the roll of mistresses immortalized by Horace. How Mrs. Sterne at first bore herself under her husband's ostentatious neglect there is no direct evidence to show. That she ultimately took refuge in indifference we can perceive, but it is to be feared that she was not always able to maintain the attitude of contemptuous composure. So, at least, we may suspect from the evidence of that Frenchman who met "le bon et agréable Tristram," and his wife, at Montpellier, and who, characteristically sympathizing with the inconstant husband, declared that his wife's incessant pursuit of him made him pass "d'assez mauvais moments," which he bore "with the patience of an angel." But, on the whole, Mrs. Sterne's conduct seems by her husband's own admissions to have been not wanting in dignity.

As to the nature of Sterne's love-affairs I have come, though not without hesitation, to the conclusion that they were most, if not all of them, what is called, somewhat absurdly, Platonic. In saying this, however, I am by no means prepared to assert that they would all of them have passed muster before a prosaic and unsentimental British jury as mere indiscretions, and nothing worse. Sterne's relations with Miss Fourmantelle, for instance, assumed at last a profoundly compromising character, and it is far from improbable that the worst construction would have

been put upon them by one of the plain-dealing tribunals
aforesaid. Certainly a young woman who leaves her
mother at York, and comes up to London to reside alone
in lodgings, where she is constantly being visited by a
lover who is himself living *en garçon* in the metropolis,
can hardly complain if her imprudence is fatal to her reputation; neither can he if his own suffers in the same
way. But, as I am not of those who hold that the con-
ventionally "innocent" is the equivalent of the morally
harmless in this matter, I cannot regard the question as
worth any very minute investigation. I am not sure that
the habitual male flirt, who neglects his wife to sit continually languishing at the feet of some other woman,
gives much less pain and scandal to others, or does much
less mischief to himself and the objects of his adoration,
than the thorough-going profligate; and I even feel tempted to risk the apparent paradox that, from the artistic
point of view, Sterne lost rather than gained by the generally Platonic character of his amours. For, as it was, the
restraint of one instinct of his nature implied the over-in-
dulgence of another which stood in at least as much need
of chastenment. If his love-affairs stopped short of the
gratification of the senses, they involved a perpetual fond-
ling and caressing of those effeminate sensibilities of his
into that condition of hyper-æsthesia which, though Sterne
regarded it as the strength, was in reality the weakness, of
his art.

Injurious, however, as was the effect which Sterne's phi-
landerings exercised upon his personal and literary character, it is not likely that, at least at this period of his life
at Sutton, they had in any degree compromised his reputation. For this he had provided in other ways, and principally by his exceedingly injudicious choice of associates.

"As to the squire of the parish," he remarks in the Memoir, "I cannot say we were on a very friendly footing, but at Stillington the family of the C[roft]s showed us every kindness: 'twas most agreeable to be within a mile and a half of an amiable family who were ever cordial friends;" and who, it may be added, appear to have been Sterne's only reputable acquaintances. For the satisfaction of all other social needs he seems to have resorted to a companionship which it was hardly possible for a clergyman to frequent without scandal—that, namely, of John Hall Stevenson and the kindred spirits whom he delighted to collect around him at Skelton—familiarly known as " Crazy " Castle. The club of the " Demoniacs," of which Sterne makes mention in his letters, may have had nothing very diabolical about it except the name ; but, headed as it was by the suspected ex-comrade of Wilkes and his brother monks of Medmenham, and recruited by gay militaires like Colonels Hall and Lee, and " fast " parsons like the Rev. " Panty " Lascelles (mock godson of Pantagruel), it was certainly a society in which the Vicar of Sutton could not expect to enroll himself without offence. We may fairly suppose, therefore, that it was to his association with these somewhat too " jolly companions" that Sterne owed that disfavour among decorous country circles, of which he shows resentful consciousness in the earlier chapters of *Tristram Shandy.*

But before we finally cross the line which separates the life of the obscure country parson from the life of the famous author, a word or two must be said of that piece of writing which was alluded to a few pages back as the only known exception to the generally " professional " character of all Sterne's compositions of the pre-Shandian era. This was a piece in the allegoric-satirical style, which,

though not very remarkable in itself, may not improbably
have helped to determine its author's thoughts in the
direction of more elaborate literary efforts. In the year
1758 a dispute had arisen between a certain Dr. Topham,
an ecclesiastical lawyer in large local practice, and Dr.
Fountayne, the then Dean of York. This dispute had
originated in an attempt on the part of the learned ci-
vilian, who appears to have been a pluralist of an exceptionally insatiable order, to obtain the reversion of one of
his numerous offices for his son, alleging a promise made
to him on that behalf by the Archbishop. This promise
—which had, in fact, been given—was legally impossible of
performance, and upon the failure of his attempt the disappointed Topham turned upon the Dean, and maintained
that by *him*, at any rate, he had been promised another
place of the value of five guineas per annum, and appro-
priately known as the " Commissaryship of Pickering and
Pocklington." This the Dean denied, and thereupon Dr.
Topham fired off a pamphlet setting forth the circumstances of the alleged promise, and protesting against the
wrong inflicted upon him by its non-performance. At
this point Sterne came to Dr. Fountayne's assistance with
a sarcastic apologue entitled the " History of a good Warm
Watchcoat," which had " hung up many years in the
parish vestry," and showing how this garment had so
excited the cupidity of Trim, the sexton, that " nothing
would serve him but he must take it home, to have it
converted into a warm under-petticoat for his wife and a
jerkin for himself against the winter." The symbolization
of Dr. Topham's snug " patent place," which he wished to
make hereditary, under the image of the good warm watchcoat, is of course plain enough ; and there is some humour
in the way in which the parson (the Archbishop) discovers

that his incautious assent to Trim's request had been given
ultra vires. Looking through the parish register, at the
request of a labourer who wished to ascertain his age, the
parson finds express words of bequest leaving the watchcoat "for the sole use of the sextons of the church for
ever, to be worn by them respectively on winterly cold
nights," and at the moment when he is exclaiming, "Just
Heaven! what an escape have I had! Give this for a
petticoat to Trim's wife!" he is interrupted by Trim himself entering the vestry with "the coat actually ript and
cut out" ready for conversion into a petticoat for his wife.
And we get a foretaste of the familiar Shandian impertinence in the remark which follows, that "there are many
good similes subsisting in the world, but which I have
neither time to recollect nor look for, which would give
you an idea of the parson's astonishment at Trim's im-
pudence." The emoluments of "Pickering and Pocklington" appear under the figure of a "pair of black velvet
plush breeches" which ultimately "got into the possession
of one Lorry Slim (Sterne himself, of course), an unlucky
wight, by whom they are still worn: in truth, as you will
guess, they are very thin by this time."

The whole thing is the very slightest of "skits;" and
the quarrel having been accommodated before it could be
published, it was not given to the world until after its
author's death. But it is interesting, as his first known
attempt in this line of composition, and the grasping sexton deserves remembrance, if only as having handed down
his name to a far more famous descendant.

CHAPTER IV.

HITHERTO we have had to construct our conception of Sterne out of materials of more or less plausible conjecture. We are now at last approaching the region of positive evidence, and henceforward, down almost to the last scene of all, Sterne's doings will be chronicled, and his character revealed, by one who happens, in this case, to be the best of all possible biographers—the man himself. Not that such records are by any means always the most trustworthy of evidence. There are some men whose real character is never more effectually concealed than in their correspondence. But it is not so with Sterne. The careless, slipshod letters which Madame de Medalle "pitchforked" into the book-market, rather than edited, are highly valuable as pieces of autobiography. They are easy, naïve, and natural, rich in simple self-disclosure in almost every page; and if they have more to tell us about the man than the writer, they are yet not wanting in instructive hints as to Sterne's methods of composition and his theories of art.

It was in the year 1759 that the Vicar of Sutton and Prebendary of York—already, no doubt, a stone of stumbling and a rock of offence to many worthy people in the

county—conceived the idea of astonishing and scandalizing
them still further after a new and original fashion. His
impulses to literary production were probably various, and
not all of them, or perhaps the strongest of them, of the
artistic order. The first and most urgent was, it may be
suspected, the simplest and most common of all such motive forces. Sterne, in all likelihood, was in want of money.
He was not, perhaps, under the actual instruction of that
magister artium whom the Roman satirist has celebrated;
for he declared, indeed, afterwards, that " he wrote not to
be fed, but to be famous." But the context of the passage
shows that he only meant to deny any absolute compul-
sion to write for mere subsistence. Between this sort of
constraint and that gentler form of pressure which arises
from the wish to increase an income sufficient for one's
needs, but inadequate to one's desires, there is a considerable difference; and to repudiate the one is not to disclaim
the other. It is, at any rate, certain that Sterne engaged
at one time of his life in a rather speculative sort of farming, and we have it from himself in a passage in one of his
letters, which may be jest, but reads more like earnest, that
it was his losses in this business that first turned his attention to literature.[1] His thoughts once set in that direction,
his peculiar choice of subject and method of treatment are
easily comprehensible. Pantagruelic burlesque came to
him, if not naturally, at any rate by " second nature."
He had a strong and sedulously cultivated taste for Rabelaisian humour; his head was crammed with all sorts of

---

[1] " I was once such a puppy myself," he writes to a certain baronet
whom he is attempting to discourage from speculative farming of
this sort, "and had my labour for my pains and two hundred pounds
out of pocket. Curse on farming! (I said). Let us see if the pen
will not succeed better than the spade."

out-of-the-way learning constantly tickling his comic sense
by its very uselessness; he relished more keenly than any
man the solemn futilities of mediæval doctors, and the pe-
dantic indecencies of casuist fathers; and, along with all
these temptations to an enterprise of the kind upon which
he entered, he had been experiencing a steady relaxation
of deterrent restraints.   He had fallen out with his uncle
some years since,[1] and the quarrel had freed him from at
least one influence making for clerical propriety of behaviour.   His incorrigible levities had probably lost him the
countenance of most of his more serious acquaintances;
his satirical humour had as probably gained him personal
enemies not a few, and it may be that he had gradually
contracted something of that "naughty-boy" temper, as
we may call it, for which the deliberate and ostentatious
repetition of offences has an inexplicable charm.   It seems
clear, too, that, growth for growth with this spirit of bravado, there had sprung up—in somewhat incongruous companionship, perhaps — a certain sense of wrong.   Along
with the impulse to give an additional shock to the preju-
dices he had already offended, Sterne felt impelled to vin-
dicate what he considered the genuine moral worth underlying the indiscretions of the offender.   What, then, could
better suit him than to compose a novel in which he might
give full play to his simious humour, startle more hideously
than ever his straighter-laced neighbours, defiantly defend
his own character, and caricature whatever eccentric figure

---

[1] He himself, indeed, makes a particular point of this in explaining
his literary venture.   "Now for your desire," he writes to a correspondent in 1759, "of knowing the reason of my turning author?
why, truly I am tired of employing my brains for other people's advantage.   'Tis a foolish sacrifice I have made for some years for an
ungrateful person."—*Letters*, i. 82.

in the society around him might offer the most tempting
butt for ridicule?

All the world knows how far he ultimately advanced
beyond the simplicity of the conception, and into what far
higher regions of art its execution led him. But I find no
convincing reason for believing that *Tristram Shandy* had
at the outset any more seriously artistic purpose than this;
and much indirect evidence that this, in fact, it was.

The humorous figure of Mr. Shandy is, of course, the
Cervantic centre of the whole ; and it was out of him and
his crotchets that Sterne, no doubt, intended from the first
to draw the materials of that often unsavoury fun which
was to amuse the light-minded and scandalize the demure.
But it can hardly escape notice that the two most elaborate portraits in Vol. I.—the admirable but very flatter-
ingly idealized sketch of the author himself in Yorick, and
the Gilrayesque caricature of Dr. Slop—are drawn with a
distinctly polemical purpose, defensive in the former case
and offensive in the latter. On the other hand, with the
disappearance of Dr. Slop caricature of living persons disappears also ; while, after the famous description of Yorick's death-bed, we meet with no more attempts at self-
vindication. It seems probable, therefore, that long before
the first two volumes were completed Sterne had discovered
the artistic possibilities of "My Uncle Toby" and "Corporal Trim," and had realized the full potentialities of humour contained in the contrast between the two brothers
Shandy. The very work of sharpening and deepening the
outlines of this humorous antithesis, while it made the
crack-brained philosopher more and more of a burlesque
unreality, continually added new touches of life and nature
to the lineaments of the simple-minded soldier ; and it was
by this curious and half-accidental process that there came

to be added to the gallery of English fiction one of the
most perfect and delightful portraits that it possesses.

We know from internal evidence that *Tristram Shandy*
was begun in the early days of 1759; and the first two
volumes were probably completed by about the middle of
the year. "In the year 1760," writes Sterne, "I went up
to London to publish my two first volumes of *Shandy*."
And it is stated in a note to this passage, as cited in Scott's
memoir, that the first edition was published "the year before" in York. There is, however, no direct proof that it
was in the hands of the public before the beginning of
1760, though it is possible that the date of its publication
may just have fallen within the year. But, at all events,
on the 1st of January, 1760, an advertisement in the *Public Advertiser* informed the world that "this day" was
"published, printed on superfine writing-paper, &c., *The
Life and Opinions of Tristram Shandy*. York. Printed
for and sold by John Hinxham, Bookseller in Stonegate."
The great London publisher, Dodsley, to whom the book
had been offered, and who had declined the venture, figures in the advertisement as the principal London bookseller from whom it was to be obtained. It seems that
only a few copies were in the first instance sent up to the
London market; but they fell into good hands, for there
is evidence that *Tristram Shandy* had attracted the notice
of at least one competent critic in the capital before the
month of January was out. But though the metropolitan
success of the book was destined to be delayed for still a
month or two, in York it had already created a *furore* in
more senses than one. For, in fact, and no wonder, it had
in many quarters given the deepest offence. Its Rabelaisian license of incident and allusion was calculated to of-
fend the proprieties—the provincial proprieties especially—

even in that free-spoken age; and there was that in the
book, moreover, which a provincial society may be count-
ed on to abominate, with a keener if less disinterested abhorrence than any sins against decency. It contained, or
was supposed to contain, a broadly ludicrous caricature of
one well-known local physician; and an allusion, brief, indeed, and covert, but highly scandalous, to a certain "droll
foible" attributed to another personage of much wider
celebrity in the scientific world. The victim in the latter
case was no longer living; and this circumstance brought
upon Sterne a remonstrance from a correspondent, to
which he replied in a letter so characteristic in many respects as to be worth quoting. His correspondent was a
Dr. * * * * * (asterisks for which it is now impossible to
substitute letters); and the burden of what seem to have
been several communications in speech and writing on the
subject was the maxim, "De mortuis nil nisi bonum."
With such seriousness and severity had his correspondent
dwelt upon this adage, that "at length," writes Sterne,
"you have made me as serious and as severe as yourself;
but, that the humours you have stirred up might not work
too potently within me, I have waited four days to cool
myself before I could set pen to paper to answer you."
And thus he sets forth the results of his four days' delib-
eration:

"'De mortuis nil nisi bonum.' I declare I have considered the
wisdom and foundation of it over and over again as dispassionately
and charitably as a good Christian can, and, after all, I can find nothing in it, or make more of it than a nonsensical lullaby of some
nurse, put into Latin by some pedant, to be chanted by some hypocrite to the end of the world for the consolation of departing lechers.
'Tis, I own, Latin, and I think that is all the weight it has, for, in
plain English, 'tis a loose and futile position below a dispute. 'You
are not to speak anything of the dead but what is good.' Why so?

Who says so ? Neither reason nor Scripture. Inspired authors have
done otherwise, and reason and common sense tell me that, if the
characters of past ages and men are to be drawn at all, they are to
be drawn like themselves, that is, with their excellences and their
foibles ; and it as much a piece of justice to the world, and to virtue,
too, to do the one as the other. The ruling passion, *et les égarements
du cœur*, are the very things which mark and distinguish a man's
character, in which I would as soon leave out a man's head as his
hobby-horse. However, if, like the poor devil of a painter, we must
conform to the pious canon, ' De mortuis,' &c., which I own has a
spice of piety in the *sound* of it, and be obliged to paint both our
angels and our devils out of the same pot, I then infer that our Syd-
enhams and our Sangrados, our Lucretias and our Messalinas, our
Somersets and our Bolingbrokes, are alike entitled to statues, and
all the historians or satirists who have said otherwise since they departed this life, from Sallust to S——e, are guilty of the crimes
you charge me with, ' cowardice and injustice.' But why cowardice ?
' Because 'tis not courage to attack a dead man who can't defend
himself.' But why do you doctors attack such a one with your incision knife ? Oh ! for the good of the living. 'Tis my plea."

And, having given this humorous twist to his argument,
he glides off into extenuatory matter. He had not even,
he protests, made as much as a surgical incision into his
victim (Dr. Richard Mead, the friend of Bentley and of
Newton, and a physician and physiologist of high repute
in his day); he had but just scratched him, and that
scarce skin-deep. As to the "droll foible" of Dr. Mead,
which he had made merry with, " it was not first reported
(even to the few who can understand the hint) by me, but
known before by every chambermaid and footman within
the bills of mortality "—a somewhat daring assertion, one
would imagine, considering what the droll foible was; and
Dr. Mead, continues Sterne, great man as he was, had,
after all, not fared worse than " a man of twice his wisdom "—to wit Solomon, of whom the same remark had

been made, that "they were both great men, and, like all
mortal men, had each their ruling passion."

The mixture of banter and sound reasoning in this reply
is, no doubt, very skilful. But, unfortunately, neither the
reasoning nor the banter happens to meet the case of this
particular defiance of the "De mortuis" maxim, and as a
serious defence against a serious charge (which was what
the occasion required) Sterne's answer is altogether futile.
For the plea of "the good of the living," upon which, after all, the whole defence, considered seriously, rests, was
quite inapplicable as an excuse for the incriminated passage. The only living persons who could possibly be affected by it, for good or evil, were those surviving friends
of the dead man, to whom Sterne's allusion to what he
called Dr. Mead's "droll foible" was calculated to cause
the deepest pain and shame.

The other matter of offence to Sterne's Yorkshire readers was of a much more elaborate kind. In the person of
Dr. Slop, the grotesque man-midwife, who was to have assisted, but missed assisting, at Tristram's entry into the
world, the good people of York were not slow to recog-
nize the physical peculiarities and professional antecedents
of Dr. Burton, the local accoucheur, whom Archdeacon
Sterne had arrested as a Jacobite. That the portrait was
faithful to anything but the external traits of the original,
or was intended to reproduce anything more than these,
Sterne afterwards denied ; and we have certainly no
ground for thinking that Burton had invited ridicule on
any other than the somewhat unworthy ground of the
curious ugliness of his face and figure. It is most unlikely
that his success as a practitioner in a branch of the medical art in which imposture is the most easily detected,
could have been earned by mere quackery ; and he seems,

moreover, to have been a man of learning in more kinds
than one.   The probability is that the worst that could
be alleged against him was a tendency to scientific pedan-
try in his published writings, which was pretty sure to
tickle the fancy of Mr. Sterne.   Unscrupulously, however,
as he was caricatured, the sensation which appears to have
been excited in the county by the burlesque portrait could
hardly have been due to any strong public sympathy with
the involuntary sitter.   Dr. Burton seems, as a suspected
Jacobite, to have been no special favourite with the Yorkshire squirearchy in general, but rather the reverse thereof.
Ucalegon, however, does not need to be popular to arouse
his neighbour's interest in his misfortunes ; and the caricature of Burton was doubtless resented on the *proximus
ardet* principle by many who feared that their turn was
coming next.

To all the complaints and protests which reached him
on the subject Sterne would in any case, probably, have
been indifferent ; but he was soon to receive encouragement which would have more than repaid a man of his
temper for twice the number of rebukes.   For London
cared nothing for Yorkshire susceptibilities and Yorkshire
fears.   Provincial notables might be libelled, and their
friends might go in fear of similar treatment, but all that
was nothing to " the town," and *Tristram Shandy* had
taken the town by storm.   We gather from a passage in
the letter above quoted that as early as January 30 the
book had " gained the very favourable opinion " of Mr.
Garrick, afterwards to become the author's intimate friend ;
and it is certain that by the time of Sterne's arrival in
London, in March, 1760, *Tristram Shandy* had become the
rage.

To say of this extraordinary work that it defies analysis

D   3   4

would be the merest inadequacy of commonplace. It was
meant to defy analysis; it is of the very essence of its
scheme and purpose that it should do so; and the mere
attempt to subject it systematically to any such process
would argue an altogether mistaken conception of the
author's intent. Its full "official" style and title is *The
Life and Opinions of Tristram Shandy, Gent.*, and it
is difficult to say which it contains the less about—the
opinions of Tristram Shandy or the events of his life. As
a matter of fact, its proper description would be "The
Opinions of Tristram Shandy's Father, with some Passages
from the Life of his Uncle." Its claim to be regarded as
a biography of its nominal hero is best illustrated by the
fact that Tristram is not born till the third volume, and
not breeched till the sixth; that it is not till the seventh
that he begins to play any active part in the narrative,
appearing then only as a completely colourless and unin-
dividualized figure, a mere vehicle for the conveyance of
Sterne's own Continental *impressions de voyage;* and that
in the last two volumes, which are entirely taken up with
the incident of his uncle's courtship, he disappears from
the story altogether. It is to be presumed, perhaps, though
not very confidently, that the reader would have seen more
of him if the tale had been continued; but how much or
how little is quite uncertain. The real hero of the book
is at the outset Mr. Shandy, senior, who is, later on, succeeded in this place of dignity by my Uncle Toby. It not
only served Sterne's purpose to confine himself mainly to
these two characters, as the best whereon to display his
powers, but it was part of his studied eccentricity to do
so. It was a "point" to give as little as possible about
Tristram Shandy in a life of Tristram Shandy; just as it
was a point to keep the reader waiting throughout the year

1760 for their hero to be so much as born. In the first
volume, therefore, the author does literally everything but
make the slightest progress with his story. Starting off
abruptly with a mock physiologic disquisition upon the
importance of a proper ordering of their mental states on
the part of the intending progenitors of children, he phi-
losophizes gravely on this theme for two or three chapters;
and then wanders away into an account of the local midwife, upon whose sole services Mrs. Shandy, in opposition
to her husband, was inclined to rely. From the midwife
it is an easy transition to her patron and protector, the
incumbent of the parish, and this, in its turn, suggests a
long excursus on the character, habits, appearance, home,
friends, enemies, and finally death, burial, and epitaph of
the Rev. Mr. Yorick. Thence we return to Mr. and Mrs.
Shandy, and are made acquainted, in absurdly minute
detail, with an agreement entered into between them with
reference to the place of sojourn to be selected for the
lady's accouchement, the burlesque deed which records
this compact being actually set out at full length. Thence,
again, we are beckoned away by the jester to join him in
elaborate and not very edifying ridicule of the Catholic
doctrine of ante-natal baptism ; and thence—but it would
be useless to follow further the windings and doublings of
this literary hare.

Yet though the book, as one thus summarizes it, may
appear a mere farrago of digressions, it nevertheless, after
its peculiar fashion, advances. Such definite purpose as
underlies the tricks and grimaces of its author is by de-
grees accomplished; and before we reach the end of the
first volume the highly humorous, if extravagantly idealized, figure of Mr. Shandy takes bodily shape and consist-
ency before our eyes. It is a mistake, I think, of Sir Wal-

ter Scott's to regard the portrait of this eccentric philosopher as intended for a satire upon perverted and deranged
erudition—as the study of a man "whom too much and
too miscellaneous learning had brought within a step or
two of madness." Sterne's conception seems to me a
little more subtle and less commonplace than that. Mr.
Shandy, I imagine, is designed to personify not "crack-
brained learning" so much as "theory run mad." He is
possessed by a sort of Demon of the Deductive, ever im-
pelling him to push his premises to new conclusions without ever allowing him time to compare them with the facts.
No doubt we are meant to regard him as a learned man;
but his son gives us to understand distinctly and very early
in the book that his crotchets were by no means those of
a weak receptive mind, overladen with more knowledge
than it could digest, but rather those of an over-active in-
telligence, far more deeply and constantly concerned with
its own processes than with the thoughts of others. Tristram, indeed, dwells pointedly on the fact that his father's
dialectical skill was not the result of training, and that he
owed nothing to the logic of the schools. "He was certainly," says his son, "irresistible both in his orations and
disputations," but that was because "he was born an orator
(Θεοδίδακτος). Persuasion hung upon his lips, and the ele-
ments of logic and rhetoric were so blended in him, and
withal he had so shrewd a guess at the weaknesses and
passions of his respondent, that Nature might have stood
up and said, 'This man is eloquent.' And yet," continues
the filial panegyric,

"He had never read Cicero nor Quintilian de Oratore, nor Aristotle,
nor Longinus among the ancients, nor Vossius, nor Skioppius, nor
Ramus, nor Farnaby among the moderns: and what is more astonishing he had never in his whole life the least light or spark of subtilty

struck into his mind by one single lecture upon Crackenthorpe or
Burgersdicius or any Dutch commentator: he knew not so much as
in what the difference of an argument *ad ignorantiam* and an argument *ad hominem* consisted; and when he went up along with me to
enter my name at Jesus College, in * * * *, it was a matter of just
wonder with my worthy tutor and two or three Fellows of that learned
society that a man who knew not so much as the names of his tools
should be able to work after that fashion with them."

Surely we all know men of this kind, and the consterna-
tion—comparable only to that of M. Jourdain under the
impromptu carte-and-tierce of his servant-maid—which
their sturdy if informal dialectic will often spread among
many kinds of "learned societies." But such men are
certainly not of the class which Scott supposed to have
been ridiculed in the character of Walter Shandy.

Among the crotchets of this born dialectician was a theory as to the importance of Christian names in determin-
ing the future behaviour and destiny of the children to
whom they are given; and, whatever admixture of jest
there might have been in some of his other fancies, in this
his son affirms he was absolutely serious. He solemnly
maintained the opinion "that there was a strange kind of
magic bias which good or bad names, as he called them,
irresistibly impressed upon our character and conduct."
How many Cæsars and Pompeys, he would say, by mere
inspiration of their names have been rendered worthy of
them! And how many, he would add, are there who might
have done exceeding well in the world had not their characters and spirits been totally depressed and Nicodemus'd
into nothing! He was astonished at parents failing to
perceive that "when once a vile name was wrongfully or
injudiciously given, 'twas not like a case of a man's character, which, when wronged, might afterwards be cleared;

and possibly some time or other, if not in the man's life,
at least after his death, be somehow or other set to rights
with the world." This name-giving injury, he would say,
"could never be undone; nay, he doubted whether an Act
of Parliament could reach it; he knew, as well as you, that
the Legislature assumed a power over surnames; but for
very strong reasons, which he could give, it had never yet
adventured, he would say, to go a step further."

With all this extravagance, however, there was combined an admirable affectation of sobriety. Mr. Shandy
would have us believe that he was no blind slave to his
theory. He was quite willing to admit the existence of
names which could not affect the character either for
good or evil — Jack, Dick, and Tom, for instance; and
such the philosopher styled "neutral names," affirming of
them, "without a satire, that there had been as many
knaves and fools at least as wise and good men since the
world began, who had indifferently borne them, so that,
like equal forces acting against each other in contrary
directions, he thought they mutually destroyed each
other's effects; for which reason he would often declare
he would not give a cherry-stone to choose among them.
Bob, which was my brother's name, was another of these
neutral kinds of Christian names which operated very little either way; and as my father happened to be at Epsom
when it was given him, he would ofttimes thank Heaven
it was no worse." Forewarned of this peculiarity of Mr.
Shandy's, the reader is, of course, prepared to hear that of
all the names in the universe the philosopher had the most
unconquerable aversion for Tristram, "the lowest and most
contemptible opinion of it of anything in the world." He
would break off in the midst of one of his frequent dis-
putes on the subject of names, and "in a spirited epipho-

nema, or rather erotesis," demand of his antagonist "whether he would take upon him to say he had ever remembered,
whether he had ever read, or whether he had ever heard
tell of a man called Tristram performing anything great or
worth recording. No, he would say. Tristram! the thing
is impossible." It only remained that he should have published a book in defence of the belief, and sure enough
"in the year sixteen," two years before the birth of his
second son, "he was at the pains of writing an express
dissertation simply upon the word Tristram, showing the
world with great candour and modesty the grounds of his
great abhorrence to the name." And with this idea Sterne
continues to amuse himself at intervals till the end of the
chapter.

That he does not so persistently amuse the reader it is,
of course, scarcely necessary to say. The jest has not substance enough—few of Sterne's jests have—to stand the
process of continual attrition to which he subjects it. But
the mere historic gravity with which the various turns of
this monomania are recorded—to say nothing of the seldom failing charm of the easy, gossiping style—prevents
the thing from ever becoming utterly tiresome. On the
whole, however, one begins to grow impatient for more of
the same sort as the three admirable chapters on the Rev.
Mr. Yorick, and is not sorry to get to the opening of the
second volume, with its half-tender, half-humorous, and
wholly delightful account of Uncle Toby's difficulties in
describing the siege operations before Namur, and of the
happy chance by which these difficulties made him ultimately the fortunate possessor of a "hobby."

Throughout this volume there are manifest signs of
Sterne's unceasing interest in his own creations, and of his
increasing consciousness of creative power. Captain Toby

Shandy is but just lightly sketched-in in the first volume,
while Corporal Trim has not made his appearance on the
scene at all; but before the end of the second we know
both of them thoroughly, within and without. Indeed, one
might almost say that in the first half-dozen chapters which
so excellently recount the origin of the corporal's fortifica-
tion scheme, and the wounded officer's delighted accept-
ance of it, every trait in the simple characters—alike yet
so different in their simplicity—of master and of man becomes definitely fixed in the reader's mind. And the total
difference between the second and the first volume in point
of fulness, variety, and colour is most marked. The artist,
the inventor, the master of dialogue, the comic dramatist,
in fact, as distinct from the humorous essayist, would almost seem to have started into being as we pass from the
one volume to the other. There is nothing in the drolleries of the first volume — in the broad jests upon Mr.
Shandy's crotchets, or even in the subtler humour of the
intellectual collision between these crotchets and his brother's plain sense—to indicate the kind of power displayed
in that remarkable colloquy _à quatre_, which begins with
the arrival of Dr. Slop and ends with Corporal Trim's recital of the Sermon on Conscience. Wit, humour, irony,
quaint learning, shrewd judgment of men and things, of
these Sterne had displayed abundance already; but it is
not in the earlier but in the later half of the first instalment of _Tristram Shandy_ that we first become conscious
that he is something more than the possessor of all these
things; that he is gifted with the genius of creation, and
has sent forth new beings into that world of immortal
shadows which to many of us is more real than our own.

CHAPTER V.

(1760–1762.)

STERNE alighted from the York mail, just as Byron "awoke
one morning," to "find himself famous." Seldom indeed
has any lion so suddenly discovered been pursued so eagerly and by such a distinguished crowd of hunters. The
chase was remarkable enough to have left a lasting impression on the spectators; for it was several years after
(in 1773) that Dr. Johnson, by way of fortifying his very
just remark that "any man who has a name or who has
the power of pleasing will be generally invited in London," observed gruffly that "the man Sterne," he was told,
"had had engagements for three months." And truly it
would appear from abundant evidence that "the man
Sterne" gained such a social triumph as might well have
turned a stronger head than his. Within twenty-four
hours after his arrival his lodgings in Pall Mall were be-
sieged by a crowd of fashionable visitors; and in a few
weeks he had probably made the acquaintance of "everybody who was anybody" in the London society of that
day.

How thoroughly he relished the delights of celebrity is

3*

revealed, with a simple vanity which almost disarms criticism, in many a passage of his correspondence. In one
of his earliest letters to Miss Fourmantelle we find him
proudly relating to her how already he "was engaged to
ten noblemen and men of fashion." Of Garrick, who had
warmly welcomed the humourist whose merits he had been
the first to discover, Sterne says that he had "promised
him at dinner to numbers of great people." Amongst
these great people who sought him out for themselves
was that discerning patron of ability in every shape, Lord
Rockingham. In one of the many letters which Madame
de Medalle flung dateless upon the world, but which from
internal evidence we can assign to the early months of
1760, Sterne writes that he is about to "set off with a
grand retinue of Lord Rockingham's (in whose suite I
move) for Windsor" to witness, it should seem, an instal-
lation of a Knight of the Garter. It is in his letters to
Miss Fourmantelle, however, that his almost boyish exulta-
tion at his London triumph discloses itself most frankly.
"My rooms," he writes, "are filling every hour with great
people of the first rank, who strive who shall most honour
me." Never, he believes, had such homage been rendered
to any man by devotees so distinguished. "The honours
paid me were the greatest that were ever known from the
great."

The self-painted portrait is not, it must be confessed,
altogether an attractive one. It is somewhat wanting in
dignity, and its air of over-inflated complacency is at times
slightly ridiculous. But we must not judge Sterne in this
matter by too severe a standard. He was by nature neither a dignified nor a self-contained man : he had a head
particularly unfitted to stand sudden elevation ; and it must
be allowed that few men's power of resisting giddiness at

previously unexplored altitudes was ever so severely tried.
It was not only "the great" in the sense of the high in
rank and social distinction by whom he was courted; he
was welcomed also by the eminent in genius and learning;
and it would be no very difficult task for him to flatter
himself that it was the latter form of recognition which
he really valued most. Much, at any rate, in the way of
undue elation may be forgiven to a country clergyman
who suddenly found himself the centre of a court, which
was regularly attended by statesmen, wits, and leaders of
fashion, and with whom even bishops condescended to
open gracious diplomatic communication. "Even all the
bishops," he writes, "have sent their compliments;" and
though this can hardly have been true of the whole Episcopal Bench, it is certain that Sterne received something
more than a compliment from one bishop, who was a host
in himself. He was introduced by Garrick to Warburton,
and received high encouragement from that formidable
prelate.[1]

The year 1760, however, was to bring to Sterne more
solid gains than that of mere celebrity, or even than the
somewhat precarious money profits which depend on literary vogue. Only a few weeks after his arrival in town
he was presented by Lord Falconberg with the curacy of
Coxwold, "a sweet retirement," as he describes it, "in
comparison of Sutton," at which he was in future to pass
most of the time spent by him in Yorkshire. What obtained him this piece of preferment is unknown. It may
be that *Tristram Shandy* drew the Yorkshire peer's atten-

[1] It is admitted, moreover, in the correspondence with Miss Fourmantelle that Sterne received something more substantial from the
Bishop, in the shape of a purse of gold; and this strange present
gave rise to a scandal on which something will be said hereafter.

tion to the fact that there was a Yorkshireman of genius
living within a few miles of a then vacant benefice in his
lordship's gift, and that this was enough for him. But
Sterne himself says—in writing a year or so afterwards to
a lady of his acquaintance—" I hope I have been of some
service to his lordship, and he has sufficiently requited me;"
and in the face of this plain assertion, confirmed as it is by
the fact that Lord Falconberg was on terms of friendly intimacy with the Vicar of Coxwold at a much later date
than this, we may dismiss idle tales about Sterne's having
" black-mailed " the patron out of a presentation to a benefice worth no more, after all, than some 70*l.* a year net.

There is somewhat more substance, however, in the
scandal which got abroad with reference to a certain alleged transaction between Sterne and Warburton. Before Sterne had been many days in London, and while
yet his person and doings were the natural subjects of the
newest gossip, a story found its way into currency to the
effect that the new-made Bishop of Gloucester had found
it advisable to protect himself against the satiric humour
of the author of the *Tristram Shandy* by a substantial
present of money. Coming to Garrick's ears, it was repeated by him—whether seriously or in jest—to Sterne,
from whom it evoked a curious letter, which in Madame
de Medalle's collection has been studiously hidden away
amongst the correspondence of seven years later. " 'Twas
for all the world," he began, " like a cut across my finger
with a sharp pen-knife. I saw the blood—gave it a suck,
wrapt it up, and thought no more about it. . . . The story
you told me of Tristram's pretended tutor this morning"
—(the scandal was, that Warburton had been threatened
with caricature in the next volume of the novel, under the
guise of the hero's tutor)—" this vile story, I say, though

I then saw both how and where it wounded, I felt little
from it at first, or, to speak more honestly (though it ruins
my simile), I felt a great deal of pain from it, but affected
an air, usual in such accidents, of feeling less than I had."
And he goes on to repudiate, it will be observed, not so
much the moral offence of corruption, in receiving money
to spare Warburton, as the intellectual solecism of select-
ing him for ridicule. "What the devil !" he exclaims, "is
there no one learned blockhead throughout the schools of
misapplied science in the Christian world to make a tutor
of for my Tristram—are we so run out of stock that there
is no one lumber-headed, muddle-headed, mortar-headed,
pudding-head chap amongst our doctors . . . but I must
disable my judgment by choosing a Warburton ?" Later
on, in a letter to his friend, Mr. Croft, at Stillington, whom
the scandal had reached through a "society journal" of
the time, he asks whether people would suppose he would
be "such a fool as to fall foul of Dr. Warburton, my best
friend, by representing him so weak a man; or by telling
such a lie of him as his giving me a purse to buy off the
tutorship of Tristram—or that I should be fool enough to
own that I had taken a purse for that purpose?" It will
be remarked that Sterne does not here deny having received a purse from Warburton, but only his having received it by way of black-mail : and the most mysterious
part of the affair is that Sterne did actually receive the
strange present of a "purse of gold" from Warburton
(whom at that time he did not know nor had ever seen);
and that he admits as much in one of his letters to Miss
Fourmantelle. "I had a purse of guineas given me yesterday by a Bishop," he writes, triumphantly, but without
volunteering any explanation of this extraordinary gift.
Sterne's letter to Garrick was forwarded, it would seem, to

Warburton; and the Bishop thanks Garrick for having procured for him "the confutation of an impertinent story the first moment I heard of it." This, however, can hardly count for much. If Warburton had really wished Sterne to abstain from caricaturing him, he would be as anxious— and for much the same reasons—to conceal the fact as to suppress the caricature. He would naturally have the disclosure of it reported to Sterne for formal contradiction, as in fulfilment of a virtual term in the bargain between them. The epithet of "irrevocable scoundrel," which he afterwards applied to Sterne, is of less importance, as proceeding from Warburton, than it would have been had it come from any one not habitually employing Warburton's peculiar vocabulary; but it at least argues no very cordial feeling on the Bishop's side. And, on the whole, one regrets to feel, as I must honestly confess that I do feel, far less confident of the groundlessness of this rather unpleasant story than could be wished. It is impossible to forget, however, that while the ethics of this matter were undoubtedly less strict in those days than they are—or, at any rate, are recognized as being—in our own, there is nothing in Sterne's character to make us suppose him to have been at all in advance of the morality of his time.

The incumbent-designate did not go down at once to take possession of his temporalities. His London triumph had not yet run its course. The first edition of Vols. I. and II. of *Tristram Shandy* was exhausted in some three months. In April, Dodsley brought out a second; and, concurrently with the advertisement of its issue, there appeared — in somewhat incongruous companionship — the announcement, "Speedily will be published, The Sermons of Mr. Yorick." The judicious Dodsley, or possibly the judicious Sterne himself (acute enough in matters of this

kind), had perceived that now was the time to publish a
series of sermons by the very unclerical lion of the day.
There would—they, no doubt, thought—be an undeniable
piquancy, a distinct flavour of semi-scandalous incongruity
in listening to the Word of Life from the lips of this loose-
tongued droll; and the more staid and serious the sermon,
the more effective the contrast.   There need not have been
much trouble in finding the kind of article required; and
we may be tolerably sure that, even if Sterne did not perceive that fact for himself, his publisher hastened to inform
him that "anything would do."   Two of his pulpit discourses, the Assize Sermon and the Charity Sermon, had
already been thought worthy of publication by their author in a separate form; and the latter of these found a
place in the series; while the rest seem to have been simply the chance sweepings of the parson's sermon-drawer.
The critics who find wit, eccentricity, flashes of Shandyism, and what not else of the same sort in these discourses,
must be able—or so it seems to me—to discover these
phenomena anywhere.   To the best of my own judgment
the Sermons are—with but few and partial exceptions—
of the most commonplace character; platitudinous with
the platitudes of a thousand pulpits, and insipid with the
crambe repetita of a hundred thousand homilies.   A single
extract will fully suffice for a specimen of Sterne's pre-
Shandian homiletic style; his post-Shandian manner was
very different, as we shall see.   The preacher is discours-
ing upon the well-worn subject of the inconsistencies of
human character:

" If such a contrast was only observable in the different stages of
a man's life, it would cease to be either a matter of wonder or of
just reproach.   Age, experience, and much reflection may naturally
enough be supposed to alter a man's sense of things, and so entirely

to transform him that, not only in outward appearance but in the
very cast and turn of his mind, he may be as unlike and different
from the man he was twenty or thirty years ago as he ever was from
anything of his own species.   This, I say, is naturally to be accounted for, and in some cases might be praiseworthy too; but the observation is to be made of men in the same period of their lives that in
the same day, sometimes on the very same action, they are utterly inconsistent and irreconcilable with themselves. Look at the man in one
light, and he shall seem wise, penetrating, discreet, and brave; behold
him in another point of view, and you see a creature all over folly
and indiscretion, weak and timorous as cowardice and indiscretion
can make him.   A man shall appear gentle, courteous, and benevolent to all mankind; follow him into his own house, maybe you see
a tyrant morose and savage to all whose happiness depends upon his
kindness.   A third, in his general behaviour, is found to be gener-
ous, disinterested, humane, and friendly.   Hear but the sad story of
the friendless orphans too credulously trusting all their whole substance into his hands, and he shall appear more sordid, more pitiless
and unjust than the injured themselves have bitterness to paint him.
Another shall be charitable to the poor, uncharitable in his censures
and opinions of all the rest of the world besides: temperate in his
appetites, intemperate in his tongue; shall have too much conscience
and religion to cheat the man who trusts him, and perhaps as far as
the business of debtor and creditor extends shall be just and scrupulous to the uttermost mite; yet in matters of full or great concern,
where he is to have the handling of the party's reputation and good
name, the dearest, the tenderest property the man has, he will do him
irreparable damage, and rob him there without measure or pity."—
Sermon XI.—*On Evil Speaking.*

There is clearly nothing particularly striking in all that,
even conveyed as it is in Sterne's effective, if loose and
careless, style; and it is no unfair sample of the whole.
The calculation, however, of the author and his shrewd
publisher was that, whatever the intrinsic merits or de-
merits of these sermons, they would "take" on the strength
of the author's name; nor, it would seem, was their calculation disappointed.   The edition of this series of sermons

now lying before me is numbered the sixth, and its date
is 1764; which represents a demand for a new edition
every nine months or so, over a space of four years. They
may, perhaps, have succeeded, too, in partially reconciling a
certain serious-minded portion of the public to the author.
Sterne evidently hoped that they might; for we find him
sending a copy to Warburton, in the month of June, immediately after the publication of the book, and receiving
in return a letter of courteous thanks, and full of excellent
advice as to the expediency of avoiding scandal by too
hazardous a style of writing in the future. Sterne, in reply, protests that he would "willingly give no offence to
mortal by anything which could look like the least viola-
tion of either decency or good manners;" but—and it is
an important "but"—he cannot promise to "mutilate everything" in *Tristram* "down to the prudish humour of
every particular" (individual), though he will do his best;
but, in any case, "laugh, my Lord, I will, and as loudly as
I can." And laugh he did, and in such Rabelaisian fashion
that the Bishop (somewhat inconsistently for a critic who
had welcomed Sterne on the appearance of the first two
volumes expressly as the "English Rabelais") remarked
of him afterwards with characteristic vigour, in a letter
to a friend, that he fears the fellow is an "irrevocable
scoundrel."

The volumes, however, which earned "the fellow" this
Episcopal benediction were not given to the world till the
next year. At the end of May or beginning of June, 1760,
Sterne went to his new home at Coxwold, and his letters
soon begin to show him to us at work upon further records
of Mr. Shandy's philosophical theory - spinning and the
simpler pursuits of his excellent brother. It is probable
that this year, 1760, was, on the whole, the happiest year

E   5

of Sterne's life. His health, though always feeble, had
not yet finally given way; and though the "vile cough"
which was to bring him more than once to death's door,
and at last to force it open, was already troubling him, he
had that within him which made it easy to bear up
against all such physical ills. His spirits, in fact, were at
their highest. His worldly affairs were going at least as
smoothly as they ever went. He was basking in that
sunshine of fame which was so delightful to a temperament differing from that of the average Englishman, as
does the physique of the Southern races from that of the
hardier children of the North; and lastly, he was exulting
in a new-born sense of creative power which no doubt
made the composition of the earlier volumes of *Tristram*
a veritable labour of love.

But the witty division of literary spinners into silk-
worms and spiders—those who spin because they are full,
and those who do so because they are empty—is not
exhaustive. There are human silk-worms who become
gradually transformed into spiders—men who begin writing in order to unburden a full imagination, and who,
long after that process has been completely performed,
continue writing in order to fill an empty belly; and
though Sterne did not live long enough to "write himself
out," there are certain indications that he would not have
left off writing if and when he felt that this stage of
exhaustion had arrived. His artistic impulses were curiously combined with a distinct admixture of the "pot-
boiler" spirit; and it was with something of the complacency of an annuitant that he looked forward to giving
the public a couple of volumes of *Tristram Shandy* every
year as long as they would stand it. In these early days,
however. there was no necessity even to discuss the prob-

able period either of the writer's inspiration or of the
reader's appetite. At present the public were as eager to
consume more Shandyism as Sterne was ready to produce
it: the demand was as active as the supply was easy. By
the end of the year Vols. III. and IV. were in the press,
and on January 27, 1761, they made their appearance.
They had been disposed of in advance to Dodsley for 380*l.*
—no bad terms of remuneration in those days; but it is
still likely enough that the publisher made a profitable
bargain. The new volumes sold freely, and the public
laughed at them as heartily as their two predecessors.
Their author's vogue in London, whither he went in December, 1760, to superintend publication, was as great
during the next spring as it had been in the last. The
tide of visitors again set in in all its former force and
volume towards the "genteel lodgings." His dinner list
was once more full, and he was feasted and flattered by
wits, beaux, courtiers, politicians, and titled-lady lion-
hunters as sedulously as ever. His letters, especially those
to his friends the Crofts, of Stillington, abound, as before,
in touches of the same amusing vanity. With how de-
licious a sense of self-importance must he have written
these words: " You made me and my friends very merry
with the accounts current at York of my being forbad the
Court, but they do not consider what a considerable person they make of me when they suppose either my going
or not going there is a point that ever enters the K.'s
head; and for those about him, I have the honour either
to stand so personally well-known to them, or to be so
well represented by those of the first rank, as to fear no
accident of the kind." Amusing, too, is it to note
the familiarity, as of an old *habitué* of Ministerial ante-
chambers, with which this country parson discusses the

political changes of that interesting year; though scarcely
more amusing, perhaps, than the solemnity with which his
daughter disguises the identity of the new Premier under
the title B——e; and by a similar use of initials attempts
to conceal the momentous state secret that the D. of R.
had been removed from the place of Groom of the Chambers, and that Sir F. D. had succeeded T. as Chancellor of
the Exchequer. Occasionally, however, the interest of his
letters changes from personal to public, and we get a
glimpse of scenes and personages that have become historical. He was present in the House of Commons at the
first grand debate on the German war after the Great
Commoner's retirement from office—"the pitched battle,"
as Sterne calls it, "wherein Mr. P. was to have entered and
thrown down the gauntlet" in defence of his military
policy. Thus he describes it:

"There never was so full a House—the gallery full to the top—I
was there all the day; when lo! a political fit of the gout seized the
great combatant—he entered not the lists. Beckford got up and
begged the House, as he saw not his right honourable friend there,
to put off the debate—it could not be done: so Beckford rose up
and made a most long, passionate, incoherent speech in defence of
the German war, but very severe upon the unfrugal manner it was
carried on, in which he addressed himself principally to the C[han-
cellor] of the E[xchequer], and laid on him terribly. . . . Legge
answered Beckford very rationally and coolly. Lord N. spoke long.
Sir F. D[ashwood] maintained the German war was most perni-
cious. . . . Lord B[arrington] at last got up and spoke half an hour
with great plainness and temper, explained many hidden things relating to these accounts in favour of the late K., and told two or
three conversations which had passed between the K. and himself
relative to these expenses, which cast great honour upon the K.'s
character. This was with regard to the money the K. had secretly
furnished out of his own pocket to lessen the account of the Han-
over-score brought us to discharge. Beckford and Barrington

abused all who fought for peace and joined in the cry for it,
and Beckford added that the reasons of wishing a peace now were
the same as at the Peace of Utrecht—that the people behind the
curtain could not both maintain the war and their places too, so
were for making another sacrifice of the nation to their own inter-
ests. After all, the cry for a peace is so general that it will certainly end in one."

And then the letter, recurring to personal matters towards the close, records the success of Vols. III. and IV.:
" One half of the town abuse my book as bitterly as the other half cry it up to the skies—the best is they abuse and
buy it, and at such a rate that we are going on with a second edition as fast as possible." This was written only in
the first week of March, so that the edition must have been
exhausted in little more than a month. It was, indeed,
another triumph; and all through this spring up to mid-
summer did Sterne remain in London to enjoy it. But,
with three distinct flocks awaiting a renewal of his pastoral
ministrations in Yorkshire, it would scarcely have done for
him, even in those easy-going days of the Establishment,
to take up his permanent abode at the capital; and early
in July he returned to Coxwold.

From the middle of this year, 1761, the scene begins to
darken, and from the beginning of the next year onward
Sterne's life was little better than a truceless struggle with
the disease to which he was destined, prematurely, to suc-
cumb. The wretched constitution which, in common with
his short-lived brothers and sisters, he had inherited probably from his father, already began to show signs of breaking up. Invalid from the first, it had doubtless been weak-
ened by the hardships of Sterne's early years, and yet
further, perhaps, by the excitements and dissipations of
his London life; nor was the change from the gaieties of

the capital to hard literary labour in a country parsonage
calculated to benefit him as much as it might others.
Shandy Hall, as he christened his pretty parsonage at Coxwold, and as the house, still standing, is called to this day,
soon became irksome to him. The very reaction begotten
of unwonted quietude acted on his temperament with a
dispiriting rather than a soothing effect. The change
from his full and stimulating life in London to the dull
round of clerical duties in a Yorkshire village might well
have been depressing to a mind better balanced and bal-
lasted than his. To him, with his light, pleasure-loving
nature, it was as the return of the schoolboy from panto-
mimes and pony-riding to the more sober delights of Dr.
Swishtail's; and, in a letter to Hall Stevenson, Sterne re-
veals his feelings with all the juvenile frankness of one of
the Doctor's pupils:

"I rejoice you are in London—rest you there in peace; here 'tis the
devil. You were a good prophet. I wish myself back again, as you
told me I should, but not because a thin, death-doing, pestiferous
north-east wind blows in a line directly from Crazy Castle turret
fresh upon me in this cuckoldly retreat (for I value the north-east
wind and all its powers not a straw), but the transition from rapid
motion to absolute rest was too violent. I should have walked about
the streets of York ten days, as a proper medium to have passed
through before I entered upon my rest; I stayed but a moment, and
I have been here but a few, to satisfy me. I have not managed my
miseries like a wise man, and if God for my consolation had not
poured forth the spirit of Shandyism unto me, which will not suffer
me to think two moments upon any grave subject, I would else just
now lay down and die."

It is true he adds, in the next sentence, that in half an
hour's time " I'll lay a guinea I shall be as merry as a
monkey, and forget it all," but such sudden revulsions of
high spirits can hardly be allowed to count for much

against the prevailing tone of discontented *ennui* which pervades this letter.

Apart, moreover, from Sterne's regrets of London, his country home was becoming from other causes a less pleasant place of abode. His relations with his wife were getting less and less cordial every year. With a perversity sometimes noticeable in the wives of distinguished men, Mrs. Sterne had failed to accept with enthusiasm the *rôle* of distant and humbly admiring spectator of her brilliant husband's triumphs. Accept it, of course, she did, being unable, indeed, to help herself; but it is clear that when Sterne returned home after one of his six months' revels in the gaieties of London, his wife, who had been vegetating the while in the retirement of Yorkshire, was not in the habit of welcoming him with effusion. Perceiving so clearly that her husband preferred the world's society to hers, she naturally, perhaps, refused to disguise her preference of her own society to his. Their estrangement, in short, had grown apace, and had already brought them to that stage of mutual indifference which is at once so comfortable and so hopeless—secure alike against the risk of " scenes " and the hope of reconciliation, shut fast in its exemption from *amantium iræ* against all possibility of *redintegratio amoris*. To such perfection, indeed, had the feeling been cultivated on both sides, that Sterne, in the letter above quoted, can write of his conjugal relations in this philosophic strain:

" As to matrimony I should be a beast to rail at it, for my wife is easy, but the world is not, and had I stayed from her a second longer it would have been a burning shame—else she declares herself happier without me. But not in anger is this declaration made (the most fatal point, of course, about it), but in pure, sober, good sense, built on sound experience. She hopes you will be able to strike a bargain for me before this twelvemonth to lead a bear round Europe, and from this hope from you I verily believe it is that you are so high in her favour at present. She swears you are a fellow of wit, though humorous ;[1] a funny, jolly soul, though somewhat splenetic, and (bating the love of women) as honest as gold. How do you like the simile ?"

There is, perhaps, a touch of affected cynicism in the suggestion that Mrs. Sterne's liking for one of her husband's friends was wholly based upon the expectation that he would rid her of her husband ; but mutual indifference must, it is clear, have reached a pretty advanced stage before such a remark could, even half in jest, be possible. And with one more longing, lingering look at the scenes which he had quitted for a lot like that of the Duke of Buckingham's dog, upon whom his master pronounced the maledictory wish that "he were married and lived in the country," this characteristic letter concludes :

"Oh, Lord ! now are you going to Ranelagh to-night, and I am sitting sorrowful as the prophet was when the voice cried out to him and said, 'What do'st thou here, Elijah ?' 'Tis well that the spirit does not make the same at Coxwold, for unless for the few sheep left me to take care of in the wilderness, I might as well, nay, better, be at Mecca. When we find we can, by a shifting of places, run away from ourselves, what think you of a jaunt there before we finally pay a visit to the Vale of Jehoshaphat ? As ill a fame as we have, I trust I shall one day or other see you face to face, so tell the two colonels if they love good company to live righteously and soberly, *as you do*, and then they will have no doubts or dangers within

---

[1] It is curious to note, as a point in the chronology of language, how exclusive is Sterne's employment of the words "humour," "humourists," in their older sense of "whimsicality," "an eccentric." The later change in its meaning gives to the word "though" in the above passage an almost comic effect.

or without them. Present my best and warmest wishes to them, and advise the eldest to prop up his spirits, and get a rich dowager before the conclusion of the peace. Why will not the advice suit both, *par nobile fratrum ?*"

In conclusion, he tells his friend that the next morning, if Heaven permit, he begins the fifth volume of *Shandy*, and adds, defiantly, that he "cares not a curse for the critics," but "will load my vehicle with what goods He sends me, and they may take 'em off my hands or let 'em alone."

The allusions to foreign travel in this letter were made with something more than a jesting intent. Sterne had already begun to be seriously alarmed, and not without reason, about the condition of his health. He shrank from facing another English winter, and meditated a southward flight so soon as he should have finished his fifth and sixth volumes, and seen them safe in the printer's hands. His publisher he had changed, for what reason is not known, and the firm of Becket & De Hondt had taken the place of Dodsley. Sterne hoped by the end of the year to be free to depart from England, and already he had made all arrangements with his ecclesiastical superiors for the necessary leave of absence. He seems to have been treated with all consideration in the matter. His Archbishop, on being applied to, at once excused him from parochial work for a year, and promised, if it should be necessary, to double that term. Fortified with this permission, Sterne bade farewell to his wife and daughter, and betook himself to London, with his now completed volumes, at the setting in of the winter. On the 21st of December they made their appearance, and in about three weeks from that date their author left England, with the intention of wintering in the South of France. There

4

were difficulties, however, of more kinds than one which
had first to be faced—a pecuniary difficulty, which Garrick met by a loan of 20*l.*, and a political difficulty, for
the removal of which Sterne had to employ the good
offices of new acquaintance later on. He reached Paris
about the 17th of January, 1762, and there met with a
reception which interposed, as might have been expected,
the most effectual of obstacles to his further progress
southward. He was received in Paris with open arms,
and stepped at once within the charmed circle of the philosophic *salons*. Again was the old intoxicating cup presented to his lips—this time, too, with more dexterous than
English hands—and again did he drink deeply of it. " My
head is turned," he writes to Garrick, " with what I see,
and the unexpected honour I have met with here. *Tristram* was almost as much known here as in London, at
least among your men of condition and learning, and has
got me introduced into so many circles ('tis *comme à
Londres*) I have just now a fortnight's dinners and suppers on my hands." We may venture to doubt whether
French politeness had not been in one respect taken somewhat too seriously by the flattered Englishman, and whether
it was much more than the name and general reputation
of *Tristram*, which was " almost as much known" in Paris
as in London. The dinners and suppers, however, were, at
any rate, no figures of speech, but very liberal entertainments, at which Sterne appears to have disported himself
with all his usual unclerical *abandon*. " I Shandy it away,"
he writes in his boyish fashion to Garrick, " fifty times
more than I was ever wont, talk more nonsense than ever
you heard me talk in all your days, and to all sorts of
people. ' Qui le diable est cet homme-là ?' said Choiseul,
t'other day, ' ce Chevalier Shandy ?' "   [We might be lis-

tening to one of Thackeray's Irish heroes.] "You'll think
me as vain as a devil was I to tell you the rest of the dialogue." But there were distinguished Frenchmen who
were ready to render to the English author more important services than that of offering him hospitality and
flattery. Peace had not been formally concluded between
France and England, and the passport with which Sterne
had been graciously furnished by Pitt was not of force
enough to dispense him from making special application
to the French Government for permission to remain in the
country. In this request he was influentially backed.
"My application," he writes, "to the Count de Choiseul
goes on swimmingly, for not only M. Pelletière (who by-
the-bye sends ten thousand civilities to you and Mrs. G.)
has undertaken my affair, but the Count de Limbourg.
The Baron d'Holbach has offered any security for the in-
offensiveness of my behaviour in France—'tis more, you
rogue! than you will do." And then the orthodox, or
professedly orthodox, English divine, goes on to describe
the character and habits of his strange new friend: "This
Baron is one of the most learned noblemen here, the great
protector of wits and of the *savans* who are no wits; keeps
open house three days a week—his house is now, as yours
was to me, my own—he lives at great expense." Equally
communicative is he as to his other great acquaintances.
Among these were the Count de Bissie, whom by an "odd
incident" (as it seemed to his unsuspecting vanity) "I
found reading *Tristram* when I was introduced to him,
which I was," he adds (without perceiving the connexion
between this fact and the "incident"), "at his desire;"
Mr. Fox and Mr. Macartney (afterwards the Lord Macartney of Chinese celebrity), and the Duke of Orleans (not
yet Égalité) himself, "who has suffered my portrait to be

added to the number of some odd men in his collection,
and has had it taken most expressively at full length by a
gentleman who lives with him." Nor was it only in the
delights of society that Sterne was now revelling. He was
passionately fond of the theatre, and his letters to Garrick
are full of eager criticism of the great French performers,
intermingled with flatteries, sometimes rather full-bodied
than delicate, of their famous English rival. Of Clairon,
in *Iphigénie*, he says " she is extremely great. Would to
God you had one or two like her. What a luxury to see
you with one of such power in the same interesting scene!
But 'tis too much." Again he writes: " The French comedy I seldom visit; they act scarce anything but tragedies;
and the Clairon is great, and Mdlle. Dumesmil in some
parts still greater than her. Yet I cannot bear preaching
—I fancy I got a surfeit of it in my younger days." And
in a later letter:

" After a vile suspension of three weeks, we are beginning with
our comedies and operas. Yours I hear never flourished more; here
the comic actors were never so low; the tragedians hold up their
heads in all senses. I have known *one little man* support the theatrical world like a David Atlas upon his shoulders, but Préville can't
do half as much here, though Mad. Clairon stands by him and sets
her back to his. She is very great, however, and highly improved
since you saw her. She also supports her dignity at table, and has
her public day every Thursday, when she gives to eat (as they say
here) to all that are hungry and dry. You are much talked of here,
and much expected, as soon as the peace will let you. These two
last days you have happened to engross the whole conversation at
the great houses where I was at dinner. 'Tis the greatest problem
in nature in this meridian that one and the same man should possess
such tragic and comic powers, and in such an *equilibrio* as to divide
the world for which of the two Nature intended him."

And while on this subject of the stage let us pause for

a moment to glance at an incident which connects Sterne
with one of the most famous of his French contemporaries. He has been asked "by a lady of talent," he tells
Garrick, "to read a tragedy, and conjecture if it would do
for you. 'Tis from the plan of Diderot; and, possibly,
half a translation of it: *The Natural Son, or the Triumph
of Virtue,* in five acts. It has too much sentiment in it
(at least for me); the speeches too long, and savour too
much of preaching. This may be a second reason it is
not to my taste—'tis all love, love, love throughout, without much separation in the characters. So I fear it would
not do for your stage, and perhaps for the very reason
which recommends it to a French one." It is curious to
see the "adaptator cerebrosuga" at work in those days as
in these; though not, in this instance, as it seems, with as
successful results. *The Natural Son, or the Triumph of
Virtue,* is not known to have reached either English readers or English theatrical audiences. The French original,
as we know, fared scarcely better. "It was not until 1771,"
says Diderot's latest English biographer, "that the direc-
tors of the French Comedy could be induced to place *Le
Fils Naturel* on the stage. The actors detested their task,
and, as we can well believe, went sulkily through parts
which they had not taken the trouble to master. The public felt as little interest in the piece as the actors had done,
and after one or two representations, it was put aside."[1]

Another, and it is to be guessed a too congenial, acquaintance formed by Sterne in Paris was that of Crébillon; and with him he concluded "a convention," unedi-
fying enough, whether in jest or earnest: "As soon as I
get to Toulouse he has agreed to write me an expostula-
tory letter upon the indecorums of *T. Shandy*, which is

[1] Morley: *Diderot and the Encyclopædists,* ii. 305.

to be answered by recrimination upon the liberties in his own works. These are to be printed together—Crébillon against Sterne, Sterne against Crébillon—the copy to be sold, and the money equally divided. This is good Swiss-policy," he adds; and the idea (which was never carried out) had certainly the merit of ingenuity, if no other.

The words "as soon as I get to Toulouse," in a letter written from Paris on the 10th of April, might well have reminded Sterne of the strange way in which he had carried out his intention of "wintering in the South." He insists, however, upon the curative effects of his winter of gaiety in Paris. "I am recovered greatly," he says; "and if I could spend one whole winter at Toulouse, I should be fortified in my inner man beyond all danger of relapsing." There was another, too, for whom this change of climate had become imperatively necessary. For three winters past his daughter Lydia, now fourteen years old, had been suffering severely from asthma, and needed to try "the last remedy of a warmer and softer air." Her father, therefore, was about to solicit passports for his wife and daughter, with a view to their joining him at once in Paris, whence, after a month's stay, they were to depart together for the South. This application for passports he intended, he said, to make "this week:" and it would seem that the intention was carried out; but, for reasons explained in a letter which Mr. Fitzgerald was the first to publish, it was not till the middle of the next month that he was able to make preparation for their joining him. From this letter—written to his Archbishop, to request an extension of his leave —we learn that while applying for the passports he was attacked with a fever, "which has ended the worst way it could for me, in a *défluxion* (*de*) *poitrine*, as the French physicians call it. It is generally fatal to weak lungs, so

that I have lost in ten days all I have gained since I came
here; and from a relaxation of my lungs have lost my
voice entirely, that 'twill be much if I ever quite recover
it. This evil sends me directly to Toulouse, for which I
set out from this place directly my family arrives." Evidently there was no time to be lost, and a week after the
date of this letter we find him in communication with Mrs.
and Miss Sterne, and making arrangements for what was,
in those days, a somewhat formidable undertaking—the
journey of two ladies from the North of England to the
centre of France. The correspondence which ensued may
be said to give us the last pleasant glimpse of Sterne's relations with his wife. One can hardly help suspecting, of
course, that it was his solicitude for the safety and comfort of his much-loved daughter that mainly inspired the
affectionate anxiety which pervades these letters to Mrs.
Sterne; but their writer is, at the very least, entitled to
credit for allowing no difference of tone to reveal itself in
the terms in which he speaks of wife and child. And,
whichever of the two he was mainly thinking of, there is
something very engaging in the thoughtful minuteness of
his instructions to the two women travellers, the earnest-
ness of his attempts to inspire them with courage for their
enterprise, and the sincere fervour of his many commen-
dations of them to the Divine keeping. The mixture of
"canny" counsel and pious invocation has frequently a
droll effect: as when the advice to "give the custom-house
officers what I told you, and at Calais more, if you have
much Scotch snuff;" and "to drink small Rhenish to keep
you cool, that is, if you like it," is rounded off by the ejac-
ulation, "So God in Heaven prosper and go along with
you!" Letter after letter did he send them, full of such
reminders as that "they have bad pins and vile needles

here," that it would be advisable to bring with them a
strong bottle-screw, and a good stout copper tea-kettle; till
at last, in the final words of preparation, his language assumes something of the solemnity of a general addressing
his army on the eve of a well-nigh desperate enterprise:
"Pluck up your spirits—trust in God, in me, and your-
selves; with this, was you put to it, you would encounter
all these difficulties ten times told. Write instantly, and
tell me you triumph over all fears—tell me Lydia is better, and a help-mate to you. You say she grows like me:
let her show me she does so in her contempt of small dangers, and fighting against the apprehensions of them, which
is better still."

At last this anxiously awaited journey was taken; and,
on Thursday, July 7, Mrs. Sterne and her daughter arrived
in Paris. Their stay there was not long—not much extended, probably, beyond the proposed week. For Sterne's
health had, some ten days before the arrival of his family,
again given him warning to depart quickly. He had but
a few weeks recovered from the fever of which he spoke
in his letter to the Archbishop, when he again broke a
blood-vessel in his lungs. It happened in the night, and
"finding in the morning that I was likely to bleed to
death, I sent immediately," he says, in a sentence which
quaintly brings out the paradox of contemporary medical
treatment, "for a surgeon to bleed me at both arms. This
saved me"—*i. e.* did not kill me—"and, with lying speech-
less three days, I recovered upon my back in bed: the
breach healed, and in a week after I got out." But the
weakness which ensued, and the subsequent "hurrying
about," no doubt as cicerone of Parisian sights to his wife
and daughter, "made me think it high time to haste to
Toulouse." Accordingly, about the 20th of the month,

and "in the midst of such heats that the oldest French-man never remembers the like," the party set off by way of Lyons and Montpellier for their Pyrenean destination. Their journey seems to have been a journey of many mis-chances, extraordinary discomfort, and incredible length; and it is not till the second week in August that we again take up the broken thread of his correspondence. Writ-ing to Mr. Foley, his banker in Paris, on the 14th of that month, he speaks of its having taken him three weeks to reach Toulouse; and adds that "in our journey we suffer-ed so much from the heats, it gives me pain to remember it. I never saw a cloud from Paris to Nismes half as broad as a twenty-four sols piece. Good God! we were toasted, roasted, grilled, stewed, carbonaded, on one side or other, all the way: and being all done through (*assez cuits*) in the day, we were eat up at night by bugs and other unswept-out vermin, the legal inhabitants, if length of possession give right, at every inn on the way." A few miles from Beaucaire he broke a hind wheel of his car-riage, and was obliged in consequence "to sit five hours on a gravelly road without one drop of water, or possibili-ty of getting any;" and here, to mend the matter, he was cursed with "two dough-hearted fools" for postilions, who "fell a-crying 'nothing was to be done!'" and could only be recalled to a worthier and more helpful mood by Sterne's "pulling off his coat and waistcoat," and "threat-ening to thrash them both within an inch of their lives."

The longest journey, however, must come to an end; and the party found much to console them at Toulouse for the miseries of travel. They were fortunate enough to se-cure one of those large, old comfortable houses which were and, here and there, perhaps, still are to be hired on the outskirts of provincial towns, at a rent which would now

F   4*   6

be thought absurdly small; and Sterne writes in terms of high complacency of his temporary abode. "Excellent," "well furnished," "elegant beyond anything I ever looked for," are some of the expressions of praise which it draws from him. He observes with pride that the "very great *salle à compagnie* is as large as Baron d'Holbach's;" and he records with great satisfaction—as well he might—that for the use of this and a country house two miles out of town, "besides the enjoyment of gardens, which the land-lord engaged to keep in order," he was to pay no more than thirty pounds a year. "All things," he adds, "are cheap in proportion: so we shall live here for a very, very little."

And this, no doubt, was to Sterne a matter of some moment at this time. The expenses of his long and tedious journey must have been heavy; and the gold-yielding vein of literary popularity, which he had for three years been working, had already begun to show signs of exhaustion. *Tristram Shandy* had lost its first vogue; and the fifth and sixth volumes, the copyright of which he does not seem to have disposed of, were "going off" but slowly.

LIFE IN THE SOUTH.——RETURN TO ENGLAND.——VOLS. VII.
AND VIII.——SECOND SET OF SERMONS.

(1762–1765.)

THE diminished appetite of the public for the humours of
Mr. Shandy and his brother is, perhaps, not very difficult
to understand. Time was simply doing its usual whole-
some work in sifting the false from the true—in ridding
Sterne's audience of its contingent of sham admirers. This
is not to say, of course, that there might not have been
other and better grounds for a partial withdrawal of popular favour. A writer who systematically employs Sterne's
peculiar methods must lay his account with undeserved
loss as well as with unmerited gain. The fifth and sixth
volumes deal quite largely enough in mere eccentricity to
justify the distaste of any reader upon whom mere eccentricity had begun to pall. But if this were the sole explanation of the book's declining popularity, we should
have to admit that the adverse judgment of the public had
been delayed too long for justice, and had passed over the
worst to light upon the less heinous offences. For the
third volume, though its earlier pages contain some good
touches, drifts away into mere dull, uncleanly equivoque in
its concluding chapters; and the fifth and sixth volumes
may, at any rate, quite safely challenge favourable compar-

ison with the fourth—the poorest, I venture to think, of
the whole series. There is nothing in these two later volumes to compare, for instance, with that 'most wearisome
exercise in *double entendre*, Slawkenbergius's Tale; nothing
to match that painfully elaborate piece of low comedy, the
consultation of philosophers and its episode of Phutatorius's mishap with the hot chestnut; no such persistent re-
sort, in short, to those mechanical methods of mirth-mak-
ing upon which Sterne, throughout a great part of the
fourth volume, almost exclusively relies. The humour of
the fifth is, to a far larger extent, of the creative and dramatic order; the ever-delightful collision of intellectual
incongruities in the persons of the two brothers Shandy
gives animation to the volume almost from beginning to
end. The arrival of the news of Bobby Shandy's death,
and the contrast of its reception by the philosophic father
and the simple-minded uncle, form a scene of inimitable
absurdity, and the "Tristrapædia," with its ingenious project for opening up innumerable "tracks of inquiry" before the mind of the pupil by sheer skill in the manipula-
tion of the auxiliary verbs, is in the author's happiest vein.
The sixth volume, again, which contains the irresistible
dialogue between Mr. and Mrs. Shandy on the great question of the "breeching of Tristram," and the much-admired,
if not wholly admirable, episode of Le Fevre's death, is fully entitled to rank beside its predecessors. On the whole,
therefore, it must be said that the colder reception accorded
to this instalment of the novel, as compared with the previous one, can hardly be justified on sound critical grounds.
But that literary shortcomings were not, in fact, the cause
of *Tristram's* declining popularity may be confidently inferred from the fact that the seventh volume, with its ad-
mirably vivid and spirited scenes of Continental travel, and

the eighth and ninth, with their charming narrative of Captain Shandy's love affair, were but slightly more successful.
The readers whom this, the third instalment of the novel,
had begun to repel, were mainly, I imagine, those who had
never felt any intelligent admiration for the former; who
had been caught by the writer's eccentricity, without ap-
preciating his insight into character and his graphic power,
and who had seen no other aspects of his humour than
those buffooneries and puerilities which, after first amusing,
had begun, in the natural course of things, to weary them.

   Meanwhile, however, and with spirits restored by the
Southern warmth to that buoyancy which never long de-
serted them, Sterne had begun to set to work upon a
new volume. His letters show that this was not the
seventh but the eighth; and Mr. Fitzgerald's conjecture,
that the materials ultimately given to the world in the former volume were originally designed for another work,
appears exceedingly probable. But for some time after
his arrival at Toulouse he was unable, it would seem, to
resume his literary labours in any form. Ever liable,
through his weakly constitution, to whatever local mala-
dies might anywhere prevail, he had fallen ill, he writes to
Hall Stevenson, "of an epidemic vile fever which killed
hundreds about me. The physicians here," he adds, "are
the arrantest charlatans in Europe, or the most ignorant of
all pretending fools. I withdrew what was left of me out
of their hands, and recommended my affairs entirely to
Dame Nature. She (dear goddess) has saved me in fifty
different pinching bouts, and I begin to have a kind of
enthusiasm now in her favour and my own, so that one or
two more escapes will make me believe I shall leave you
all at last by translation, and not by fair death." Having
now become " stout and foolish again as a man can wish

to be, I am," he says, " busy playing the fool with my
Uncle Toby, whom I have got soused over head and ears
in love." Now, it is not till the eighth volume that the
Widow Wadman begins to weave her spells around Captain Shandy's ingenuous heart ; while the seventh volume
is mainly composed of that series of travel-pictures in
which Sterne has manifestly recorded his own impressions
of Northern France in the person of the youthful Tristram.
It is scarcely doubtful, therefore, that it is these sketches,
and the use which he then proposed to make of them, that
he refers to, when speaking in this letter of " hints and
projects for other works." Originally intended to form a
part of the volume afterwards published as the *Sentimental
Journey*, it was found necessary—under pressure, it is to be
supposed, of insufficient matter—to work them up instead
into an interpolated seventh volume of *Tristram Shandy*.
At the moment, however, he no doubt as little foresaw this
as he did the delay which was to take place before any
continuation of the novel appeared. He clearly contem-
plated no very long absence from England. " When I
have reaped the benefit of the winter at Toulouse, I cannot
see I have anything more to do with it. Therefore, after
having gone with my wife and girl to Bagnères, I shall
return from whence I came." Already, however, one can
perceive signs of his having too presumptuously marked
out his future. " My wife wants to stay another year, to
save money ; and this opposition of wishes, though it will
not be as sour as lemon, yet 'twill not be as sweet as
sugar." And again : " If the snows will suffer me, I propose to spend two or three months at Barége or Bagnères ;
but my dear wife is against all schemes of additional expense, which wicked propensity (though not of despotic
power) yet I cannot suffer—though, by-the-bye, laudable

enough. But she may talk; I will go my own way, and she will acquiesce without a word of debate on the subject. Who can say so much in praise of his wife? Few, I trow." The tone of contemptuous amiability shows pretty clearly that the relations between husband and wife had in nowise improved. But wives do not always lose all their influence over husbands' wills along with the power over their affections; and it will be seen that Sterne did *not* make his projected winter trip to Bagnères, and that he did remain at Toulouse for a considerable part of the second year for which Mrs. Sterne desired to prolong their stay. The place, however, was not to his taste; and he was not the first traveller in France who, delighted with the gaiety of Paris, has been disappointed at finding that French provincial towns can be as dull as dulness itself could require. It is in the somewhat unjust mood which is commonly begotten of disillusion that Sterne discovers the cause of his *ennui* in "the eternal platitude of the French character," with its "little variety and no originality at all." " They are very civil," he admits, " but civility itself so thus uniform wearies and bothers me to death. If I do not mind I shall grow most stupid and sententious." With such apprehensions it is not surprising that he should have eagerly welcomed any distraction that chance might offer, and in December we find him joyfully informing his chief correspondent of the period, Mr. Foley—who to his services as Sterne's banker seems to have added those of a most helpful and trusted friend—that " there are a company of English strollers arrived here who are to act comedies all the Christmas, and are now busy in making dresses and preparing some of our best comedies." These so-called strollers were, in fact, certain members of the English colony in Toulouse, and their performances were

among the first of those "amateur theatrical" entertainments which now-a-days may be said to rival the famous
"morning drum-beat" of Daniel Webster's oration, in
marking the ubiquity of British boredom, as the *reveil*
does that of British power over all the terrestrial globe.
"The next week," writes Sterne, "with a grand orchestra,
we play *The Busybody*, and the *Journey to London* the
week after; but I have some thought of adapting it to
our situation, and making it the *Journey to Toulouse*,
which, with the change of half-a-dozen scenes, may be
easily done. Thus, my dear Foley, for want of something
better we have recourse to ourselves, and strike out the
best amusements we can from such materials." "Recourse to ourselves," however, means, in strict accuracy,
"recourse to each other;" and when the amateur players
had played themselves out, and exhausted their powers of
contributing to each others' amusement, it is probable that
"recourse to ourselves," in the exact sense of the phrase,
was found ineffective—in Sterne's case, at any rate—to
stave off *ennui*. To him, with his copiously if somewhat
oddly furnished mind, and his natural activity of imagination, one could hardly apply the line of Persius,

"Tecum habita et noris quam sit tibi curta supellex;"

but it is yet evident enough that Sterne's was one of that
numerous order of intellects which are the convivial associates, rather than the fireside companions, of their own-
ers, and which, when deprived of the stimulus of external
excitement, are apt to become very dull company indeed.
Nor does he seem to have obtained much diversion of
mind from his literary work—a form of intellectual enjoyment which, indeed, more often presupposes than begets good spirits in such temperaments as his. He de-

clares, it is true, that he "sports much with my Uncle
Toby" in the volume which he is now "fabricating for
the laughing part of the world;" but if so he must have
sported only after a very desultory and dilatory fashion.
On the whole one cannot escape a very strong impression
that Sterne was heartily bored by his sojourn in Toulouse,
and that he eagerly longed for the day of his return to
"the dalliance and the wit, the flattery and the strife,"
which he had left behind him in the two great capitals in
which he had shone.

His stay, however, was destined to be very prolonged.
The winter of 1762 went by, and the succeeding year had
run nearly half its course, before he changed his quarters.
"The first week in June," he writes in April to Mr. Foley,
"I decamp like a patriarch, with all my household, to pitch
our tents for three months at the foot of the Pyrenean
hills at Bagnères, where I expect much health and much
amusement from all corners of the earth." He talked too
at this time of spending the winter at Florence, and, after
a visit to Leghorn, returning home the following April by
way of Paris; "but this," he adds, "is a sketch only,"
and it remained only a sketch. Toulouse, however, he
was in any case resolved to quit. He should not, he said,
be tempted to spend another winter there. It did not suit
his health, as he had hoped: he complained that it was too
moist, and that he could not keep clear of ague. In June,
1763, he quitted it finally for Bagnères; whence after a
short, and, as we subsequently learn, a disappointed, sojourn, he passed on to Marseilles, and later to Aix, for
both of which places he expressed dislike; and by October he had gone again into winter quarters at Montpellier,
where "my wife and daughter," he writes, "purpose to
stay at least a year behind me." His own intention was

to set out in February for England, " where my heart has
been fled these six months." Here again, however, there
are traces of that periodic, or rather, perhaps, that chronic
conflict of inclination between himself and Mrs. Sterne, of
which he speaks with such a tell-tale affectation of philosophy. " My wife," he writes in January, " returns to Toulouse, and proposes to spend the summer at Bagnères. I,
on the contrary, go to visit my wife the church in Yorkshire. We all live the longer, at least the happier, for
having things our own way. This is my conjugal maxim.
I own 'tis not the best of maxims, but I maintain 'tis not
the worst." It was natural enough that Sterne, at any rate,
should wish to turn his back on Montpellier. Again had
the unlucky invalid been attacked by a dangerous illness;
the " sharp air " of the place disagreed with him, and his
physicians, after having him under their hands more than
a month, informed him coolly that if he stayed any longer
in Montpellier it would be fatal to him. How soon after
that somewhat late warning he took his departure there
is no record to show; but it is not till the middle of May
that we find him writing from Paris to his daughter. And
since he there announces his intention of leaving for England in a few days, it is a probable conjecture that he had
arrived at the French capital some fortnight or so before.

His short stay in Paris was marked by two incidents—
trifling in themselves, but too characteristic of the man to
be omitted. Lord Hertford, the British Ambassador, had
just taken a magnificent hotel in Paris, and Sterne was
asked to preach the first sermon in its chapel. The message was brought him, he writes, " when I was playing a
sober game of whist with Mr. Thornhill; and whether I
was called abruptly from my afternoon amusement to pre-
pare myself for the business on the next day, or from what

other cause, I do not pretend to determine; but that unlucky kind of fit seized me which you know I am never
able to resist, and a very unlucky text did come into my
head." The text referred to was 2 Kings xx. 15—Heze-
kiah's admission of that ostentatious display of the treas-
ures of his palace to the ambassadors of Babylon for which
Isaiah rebuked him by prophesying the Babylonian captivity of Judah. Nothing, indeed, as Sterne protests, could
have been more innocent than the discourse which he
founded upon the *mal-à-propos* text; but still it was unquestionably a fair subject for "chaff," and the preacher
was rallied upon it by no less a person than David Hume.
Gossip having magnified this into a dispute between the
parson and the philosopher, Sterne disposes of the idle
story in a passage deriving an additional interest from its
tribute to that sweet disposition which had an equal charm
for two men so utterly unlike as the author of *Tristram
Shandy* and the author of the *Wealth of Nations.* "I
should," he writes, "be exceedingly surprised to hear that
David ever had an unpleasant contention with any man;
and if I should ever be made to believe that such an event
had happened, nothing would persuade me that his oppo-
nent was not in the wrong, for in my life did I never meet
with a being of a more placid and gentle nature; and it is
this amiable turn of his character which has given more
consequence and force to his scepticism than all the argu-
ments of his sophistry." The real truth of the matter
was that, meeting Sterne at Lord Hertford's table on the
day when he had preached at the Embassy Chapel, "David
was disposed to make a little merry with the parson, and
in return the parson was equally disposed to make a little
merry with the infidel. We laughed at one another, and
the company laughed with us both." It would be absurd,

of course, to identify Sterne's latitudinarian *bonhomie* with
the higher order of tolerance; but many a more confirmed
and notorious Gallio than the clerical humourist would
have assumed prudish airs of orthodoxy in such a presence, and the incident, if it does not raise one's estimate
of Sterne's dignity, displays him to us as laudably free
from hypocrisy.

But the long holiday of somewhat dull travel, with its
short last act of social gaiety, was drawing to a close. In
the third or fourth week of May Sterne quitted Paris; and
after a stay of a few weeks in London he returned to the
Yorkshire parsonage, from which he had been absent some
thirty months.

Unusually long as was the interval which had elapsed
since the publication of the last instalment of *Tristram
Shandy*, the new one was far from ready; and even in
the "sweet retirement" of Coxwold he seems to have
made but slow progress with it. Indeed, the "sweet retirement" itself became soon a little tedious to him. The
month of September found him already bored with work
and solitude; and the fine autumn weather of 1764 set
him longing for a few days' pleasure-making at what was
even then the fashionable Yorkshire watering-place. "I
do not think," he writes, with characteristic incoherence,
to Hall Stevenson—"I do not think a week or ten days'
playing the good fellow (at this very time) so abominable
a thing; but if a man could get there cleverly, and every
soul in his house in the mind to try what could be done
in furtherance thereof, I have no one to consult in these
affairs. Therefore, as a man may do worse things, the
plain English of all which is, that I am going to leave a
few poor sheep in the wilderness for fourteen days, and
from pride and naughtiness of heart to go see what is

doing at Scarborough, steadfully meaning afterwards to lead a new life and strengthen my faith. Now, some folks say there is much company there, and some say not; and I believe there is neither the one nor the other, but will be both if the world will have patience for a month or so." Of his work he has not much to say : " I go on not rapidly but well enough with my Uncle Toby's amours. There is no sitting and cudgelling one's brains whilst the sun shines bright. 'Twill be all over in six or seven weeks ; and there are dismal weeks enow after to endure suffocation by a brimstone fireside." He was anxious that his boon companion should join him at Scarborough ; but that additional pleasure was denied him, and he had to content himself with the usual gay society of the place. Three weeks, it seems, were passed by him in this most doubtfully judicious form of bodily and mental relaxation —weeks which he spent, he afterwards writes, in " drinking the waters, and receiving from them marvellous strength, had I not debilitated it as fast as I got it by playing the good fellow with Lord Granby and Co. too much." By the end of the month he was back again at Coxwold, " returned to my Philosophical Hut to finish *Tristram*, which I calculate will be ready for the world about Christmas, at which time I decamp from hence and fix my headquarters at London for the winter, unless my cough pushes me forward to your metropolis " (he is writing to Foley, in Paris), " or that I can persuade some *gros milord* to make a trip to you." Again, too, in this letter we get another glimpse at that thoroughly desentimentalized " domestic interior " which the sentimentalist's household had long presented to the view. Writing to request a remittance of money to Mrs. Sterne at Montauban—a duty which, to do him justice, he seems to have very watchfully

observed—Sterne adds his solicitation to Mr. Foley to "do
something equally essential to rectify a mistake in the
mind of your correspondent there, who, it seems, gave her
a hint not long ago 'that she was separated from me for
life.' Now, as this is not true, in the first place, and may
fix a disadvantageous impression of her to those she lives
amongst, 'twould be unmerciful to let her or my daughter
suffer by it. So do be so good as to undeceive him; for
in a year or two she purposes (and I expect it with impatience from her) to rejoin me."

Early in November the two new volumes of *Shandy* began to approach completion; for by this time Sterne had
already made up his mind to interpolate these notes of his
French travels, which now do duty as Vol. VII. "You
will read," he tells Foley, "as odd a tour through France
as was ever projected or executed by traveller or travel-
writer since the world began. 'Tis a laughing, good-tem-
pered satire upon travelling—as *puppies* travel." By the
16th of the month he had "finished my two volumes
of *Tristram*," and looked to be in London at Christmas,
"whence I have some thoughts of going to Italy this year.
At least I shall not defer it above another." On the 26th
of January, 1765, the two new volumes were given to the
world.

Shorter in length than any of the preceding instalments,
and filled out as it was, even so, by a process of what
would now be called "book-making," this issue will yet
bear comparison, I think, with the best of its predecessors.
Its sketches of travel, though destined to be surpassed in
vigour and freedom of draftsmanship by the *Sentimental
Journey*, are yet excellent, and their very obvious want of
connexion with the story—if story it can be called—is so
little felt that we almost resent the head-and-ears introduc-

tion of Mr. Shandy and his brother, and the Corporal, in
apparent concession to the popular prejudice in favour of
some sort of coherence between the various parts of a narrative. The first seventeen chapters are, perhaps, as freshly
delightful reading as anything in Sterne. They are literally filled and brimming over with the exhilaration of
travel: written, or at least prepared for writing, we can
clearly see, under the full intoxicant effect which a bewil-
dering succession of new sights and sounds will produce,
in a certain measure, upon the coolest of us, and which
would set a head like Sterne's in an absolute whirl. The
contagion of his high spirits is, however, irresistible; and,
putting aside all other and more solid qualities in them,
these chapters are, for mere fun—for that kind of clever
nonsense which only wins by perfect spontaneity, and
which so promptly makes ashamed the moment spontaneity fails—unsurpassed by anything of the same kind
from the same hand. How strange, then, that, with so
keen an eye for the humorous, so sound and true a judgment in the highest qualities of humour, Sterne should
think it possible for any one who has outgrown what may
be called the dirty stage of boyhood to smile at the story
which begins a few chapters afterwards — that of the
Abbess and Novice of the Convent of Andouillets! The
adult male person is not so much shocked at the coarseness of this story as astounded at the bathos of its introduction. It is as though some matchless connoisseur in
wine, after having a hundred times demonstrated the unerring discrimination of his palate for the finest brands,
should then produce some vile and loaded compound, and
invite us to drink it with all the relish with which he
seems to be swallowing it himself. This story of the Abbess and Novice almost impels us to turn back to certain

earlier chapters, or former volumes, and re-examine some
of the subtler passages of humour to be found there—in
downright apprehension lest we should turn out to have
read these "good things," not "in," but "into," our author. The bad wine is so very bad, that we catch ourselves wondering whether the finer brands were genuine,
when we see the same palate equally satisfied with both.
But one should, of course, add that it is only in respect of
its supposed humour that this story shakes its readers'
faith in the gifts of the narrator. As a mere piece of
story-telling, and even as a study in landscape and figure-
painting, it is quite perversely skilful. There is something
almost irritating, as a waste of powers on unworthy material, in the prettiness of the picture which Sterne draws
of the preparations for the departure of the two *religieuses*
—the stir in the simple village, the co-operating labours of
the gardener and the tailor, the carpenter and the smith,
and all those other little details which bring the whole
scene before the eye so vividly that Sterne may, perhaps,
in all seriousness, and not merely as a piece of his characteristic persiflage, have thrown in the exclamation, "I declare I am interested in this story, and wish I had been
there." Nothing, again, could be better done than the
sketch of the little good-natured, "broad-set" gardener,
who acted as the ladies' muleteer, and the recital of the
indiscretions by which he was betrayed into temporary de-
sertion of his duties. The whole scene is Chaucerian in
its sharpness of outline and translucency of atmosphere:
though there, unfortunately, the resemblance ends. Sterne's
manner of saying what we now leave unsaid is as unlike
Chaucer's, and as unlike for the worse, as it can possibly be.

Still, a certain amount of this element of the *non nomi-*

nandum must be compounded for, one regrets to say, in
nearly every chapter that Sterne ever wrote; and there
is certainly less than the average amount of it in the
seventh volume. Then, again, this volume contains the
famous scene with the ass—the live and genuinely touching, and not the dead and fictitiously pathetic, animal;
and that perfect piece of comic dialogue—the interview
between the puzzled English traveller and the French commissary of the posts. To have suggested this scene is, perhaps, the sole claim of the absurd fiscal system of the *An-
cien régime* upon the grateful remembrance of the world.
A scheme of taxation which exacted posting-charges from
a traveller who proposed to continue his journey by water,
possesses a natural ingredient of drollery infused into its
mere vexatiousness; but a whole volume of satire could
hardly put its essential absurdity in a stronger light than
is thrown upon it in the short conversation between the
astonished Tristram and the officer of the fisc, who had
just handed him a little bill for six livres four sous:

"'Upon what account?' said I.

"''Tis upon the part of the King,' said the commissary, heaving
up his shoulders.

"'My good friend,' quoth I, 'as sure as I am I, and you are you—'

"'And who are you?' he said.

"'Don't puzzle me,' said I. 'But it is an indubitable verity,' I
continued, addressing myself to the commissary, changing only the
form of my asseveration, 'that I owe the King of France nothing but
my good-will, for he is a very honest man, and I wish him all the health
and pastime in the world.'

"'Pardonnez-moi,' replied the commissary. 'You are indebted to
him six livres four sous for the next post from hence to St. Fons, on
your route to Avignon, which being a post royal, you pay double for
the horses and postilion, otherwise 'twould have amounted to no more
than three livres two sous.'

"'But I don't go by land,' said I.

G   5   7

" ' You may if you please,' replied the commissary.

" ' Your most obedient servant,' said I, making him a low bow.

"The commissary, with all the sincerity of grave good-breeding, made me one as low again. I never was more disconcerted by a bow in my life. 'The devil take the serious character of these people,' said I, aside; 'they understand no more of irony than this.' The comparison was standing close by with her panniers, but something sealed up my lips. I could not pronounce the name.

" ' Sir,' said I, collecting myself, 'it is not my intention to take post.'

" ' But you may,' said he, persisting in his first reply. 'You may if you choose.'

" ' And I may take salt to my pickled herring if I choose.[1] But I do not choose.'

" ' But you must pay for it, whether you do or no.'

" ' Ay, for the salt,' said I, 'I know.'

" ' And for the post, too,' added he.

" ' Defend me !' cried I. 'I travel by water. I am going down the Rhone this very afternoon; my baggage is in the boat, and I have actually paid nine livres for my passage.'

" ' C'est tout égal—'tis all one,' said he.

" ' Bon Dieu ! What ! pay for the way I go and for the way I do not go ?'

" ' C'est tout égal,' replied the commissary.

" ' The devil it is !' said I. 'But I will go to ten thousand Bastilles first. O, England ! England ! thou land of liberty and climate of good-sense ! thou tenderest of mothers and gentlest of nurses !' cried

---

[1] It is the penalty—I suppose the just penalty—paid by habitually extravagant humourists, that *meaning* not being always expected of them, it is not always sought by their readers with sufficient care. Anyhow, it may be suspected that this retort of Tristram's is too often passed over as a mere random absurdity designed for his interlocutor's mystification, and that its extremely felicitous pertinence to the question in dispute is thus overlooked. The point of it, of course, is that the business in which the commissary was then engaged was precisely analogous to that of exacting salt dues from perverse persons who were impoverishing the revenue by possessing herrings already pickled.

I, kneeling upon one knee as I was beginning my apostrophe—when the director of Madame L. Blanc's conscience coming in at that instant, and seeing a person in black, with a face as pale as ashes, at his devotions, asked if I stood in want of the aids of the Church.

"'I go by water,' said I, 'and here's another will be for making me pay for going by oil.'"

The commissary, of course, remains obdurate, and Tristram protests that the treatment to which he is being subjected is "contrary to the law of nature, contrary to reason, contrary to the Gospel:"

"'But not to this,' said he, putting a printed paper into my hand. "'De par le Roi.' ''Tis a pithy prolegomenon,' quoth I, and so read on. . . . 'By all which it appears,' quoth I, having read it over a little too rapidly, 'that if a man sets out in a post-chaise for Paris, he must go on travelling in one all the days of his life, or pay for it.' "'Excuse me,' said the commissary, 'the spirit of the ordinance is this, that if you set out with an intention of running post from Paris to Avignon, &c., you shall not change that intention or mode of travelling without first satisfying the fermiers for two posts further than the place you repent at; and 'tis founded,' continued he, 'upon this, that the revenues are not to fall short through your fickleness.' "'O, by heavens!' cried I, 'if fickleness is taxable in France, we have nothing to do but to make the best peace we can.' "And so the peace was made."

And the volume ends with the dance of villagers on "the road between Nismes and Lunel, where is the best Muscatto wine in all France"—that charming little idyll which won the unwilling admiration of the least friendly of Sterne's critics.[1]

With the close of this volume the shadowy Tristram disappears altogether from the scene; and even the clearly-sketched figures of Mr. and Mrs. Shandy recede somewhat into the background. The courtship of my Uncle

[1] Thackeray: *English Humourists*, vol. x. p. 568, ed. 1879.

Toby forms the whole *motif*, and indeed almost the entire
substance, of the next volume. Of this famous episode
in the novel a great deal has been said and written, and
much of the praise bestowed upon it is certainly deserved.
The artful coquetries of the fascinating widow, and the
gradual capitulation of the Captain, are studied with admirable power of humorous insight, and described with infinite grace and skill. But there is, perhaps, no episode in
the novel which brings out what may be called the perversity of Sterne's animalism in a more exasperating way.
It is not so much the amount of this element as the time,
place, and manner in which it makes its presence felt. The
senses must, of course, play their part in all love affairs, except those of the angels—or the triangles; and such writers
as Byron, for instance, are quite free from the charge of
over-spiritualizing their description of the passion. Yet
one might safely say that there is far less to repel a
healthy mind in the poet's account of the amour of Juan
and Haidee than is to be found in many a passage in this
volume. It is not merely that one is the poetry and the
other the prose of the sexual passion : the distinction goes
deeper, and points to a fundamental difference of attitude
towards their subject in the two writers' minds.

The success of this instalment of *Tristram Shandy* appears to have been slightly greater than that of the preceding one. Writing from London, where he was once
more basking in the sunshine of social popularity, to Garrick, then in Paris, he says (March 16, 1765): "I have had
a lucrative campaign here. *Shandy* sells well," and "I am
taxing the public with two more volumes of sermons, which
will more than double the gains of *Shandy*. It goes into
the world with a prancing list *de toute la noblesse*, which
will bring me in three hundred pounds, exclusive of the

sale of the copy." The list was, indeed, extensive and distinguished enough to justify the curious epithet which he applies to it; but the cavalcade of noble names continued to "prance" for some considerable time without advancing. Yet he had good reasons, according to his own account, for wishing to push on their publication. His parsonage-house at Sutton had just been burnt down through the carelessness of one of his curate's household, with a loss to Sterne of some 350*l*. "As soon as I can," he says, "I must rebuild it, but I lack the means at present." Nevertheless, the new sermons continued to hang fire. Again, in April he describes the subscription list as "the most splendid list which ever pranced before a book since subscription came into fashion;" but though the volumes which it was to usher into the world were then spoken of as about to be printed "very soon," he has again in July to write of them only as "forthcoming in September, though I fear not in time to bring them with me" to Paris. And, as a matter of fact, they do not seem to have made their appearance until after Sterne had quitted England on his second and last Continental journey. The full subscription list may have had the effect of relaxing his energies; but the subscribers had no reason to complain when, in 1766, the volumes at last appeared.

The reception given to the first batch of sermons which Sterne had published was quite favourable enough to encourage a repetition of the experiment. He was shrewd enough, however, to perceive that on this second occasion a somewhat different sort of article would be required. In the first flush of *Tristram Shandy's* success, and in the first piquancy of the contrast between the grave profession of the writer and the unbounded license of the book, he could safely reckon on as large and curious a public for *any*

sermons whatever from the pen of Mr. Yorick. There
was no need that the humourist in his pulpit should at all
resemble the humourist at his desk, or, indeed, that he
should be in any way an impressive or commanding figure.
The great desire of the world was to know what he *did*
resemble in this new and incongruous position. Men
wished to see what the queer, sly face looked like over
a velvet cushion, in the assurance that the sight would be
a strange and interesting one, at any rate. Five years afterwards, however, the case was different. The public then
had already had one set of sermons, and had discovered
that the humorous Mr. Sterne was not a very different man
in the pulpit from the dullest and most decorous of his
brethren. Such discoveries as these are instructive to
make, but not attractive to dwell upon; and Sterne was
fully alive to the probability that there would be no great
demand for a volume of sermons which should only illus-
trate for the second time the fact that he could be as commonplace as his neighbour. He saw that in future the
Rev. Mr. Yorick must a little more resemble the author of
Tristram Shandy, and it is not improbable that from 1760
onwards he composed his parochial sermons with especial
attention to this mode of qualifying them for republication.
There is, at any rate, no slight critical difficulty in believing that the bulk of the sermons of 1766 can be assigned
to the same literary period as the sermons of 1761. The
one set seems as manifestly to belong to the post-Shandian
as the other does to the pre-Shandian era; and in some,
indeed, of the apparently later productions the daring
quaintness of style and illustration is carried so far that,
except for the fact that Sterne had no time to spare for
the composition of sermons not intended for professional
use, one would have been disposed to believe that they

neither were nor were meant to be delivered from the pulpit at all.[1]   Throughout all of them, however, Sterne's
new-found literary power displays itself in a vigour of expression and vivacity of illustration which at least serve to
make the sermons of 1766 considerably more entertain-
ing reading than those of 1761.   In the first of the latter
series, for instance—the sermon on Shimei—a discourse
in which there are no very noticeable sallies of unclerical
humour, the quality of liveliness is very conspicuously
present.   The preacher's view of the character of Shimei,
and of his behaviour to David, is hardly that, perhaps, of
a competent historical critic, and in treating of the Ben-
jamite's insults to the King of Israel he appears to take
no account of the blood-feud between the house of David
and the clan to which the railer belonged; just as in commenting on Shimei's subsequent and most abject submis-
sion to the victorious monarch, Sterne lays altogether too
much stress upon conduct which is indicative, not so much
of any exceptional meanness of disposition, as of the ordinary suppleness of the Oriental put in fear of his life.
However, it makes a more piquant and dramatic picture to
represent Shimei as a type of the wretch of insolence and
servility compact, with a tongue ever ready to be loosed
against the unfortunate, and a knee ever ready to be bent
to the strong.   And thus he moralizes on his conception:

"There is not a character in the world which has so bad an influence upon it as this of Shimei. While power meets with honest
checks, and the evils of life with honest refuge, the world will never
be undone; but thou, Shimei, hast sapped it at both extremes: for
thou corruptest prosperity, and 'tis thou who hast broken the heart

---

[1] Mr. Fitzgerald, indeed, asserts as a fact that some at least of
these sermons were actually composed in the capacity of *littérateur*
and not of divine—for the press and not for the pulpit.

of poverty. And so long as worthless spirits can be ambitious ones
'tis a character we never shall want. Oh! it infests the court, the
camp, the cabinet; it infests the Church. Go where you will, in
every quarter, in every profession, you see a Shimei following the
wheels of the fortunate through thick mire and clay. Haste, Shimei,
haste! or thou wilt be undone forever. Shimei girdeth up his loins
and speedeth after him. Behold the hand which governs everything
takes the wheel from his chariot, so that he who driveth, driveth on
heavily. Shimei doubles his speed; but 'tis the contrary way: he flies
like the wind over a sandy desert. . . . Stay, Shimei! 'tis your patron,
your friend, your benefactor, the man who has saved you from the
dunghill. 'Tis all one to Shimei. Shimei is the barometer of every
man's fortune; marks the rise and fall of it, with all the variations
from scorching hot to freezing cold upon his countenance that the
simile will admit of.[1] Is a cloud upon thy affairs? See, it hangs
over Shimei's brow! Hast thou been spoken for to the king or the
captain of the host without success? Look not into the Court Cal-
endar, the vacancy is filled in Shimei's face. Art thou in debt, though
not to Shimei? No matter. The worst officer of the law shall not
be more insolent. What, then, Shimei, is the fault of poverty so
black? is it of so general concern that thou and all thy family must
rise up as one man to reproach it? When it lost everything, did it
lose the right to pity too? Or did he who maketh poor as well as
maketh rich strip it of its natural powers to mollify the heart and
supple the temper of your race? Trust me you have much to answer for. It is this treatment which it has ever met with from spirits like yours which has gradually taught the world to look upon it
as the greatest of evils, and shun it as the worst disgrace. And what
is it, I beseech you—what is it that men will not do to keep clear of
so sore an imputation and punishment? Is it not to fly from this
that he rises early, late takes rest, and eats the bread of carefulness?
that he plots, contrives, swears, lies, shuffles, puts on all shapes, tries
all garments, wears them with this or that side outward, just as it
may favour his escape?"

And though the sermon ends in orthodox fashion, with
an assurance that, in spite of the Shimeis by whom we

[1] Which are not many in the case of a *barometer*.

are surrounded, it is in our power to "lay the foundation
of our peace (where it ought to be) within our own
hearts," yet the preacher can, in the midst of his earlier
reflections, permit himself the quaintly pessimistic out-
burst: "O Shimei! would to Heaven, when thou wast
slain, that all thy family had been slain with thee, and
not one of thy resemblance left! But ye have multiplied
exceedingly, and replenished the earth; and if I prophesy
rightly, ye will in the end subdue it."

Nowhere, however, does the man of the world reveal
himself with more strangely comical effect under the
gown of the divine than in the sermon on "The Prodigal Son." The repentant spendthrift has returned to
his father's house, and is about to confess his follies.
But—

"Alas! How shall he tell his story?

"Ye who have trod this round, tell me in what words he shall give
in to his father the sad items of his extravagance and folly: the
feasts and banquets which he gave to whole cities in the East; the
costs of Asiatic rarities, and of Asiatic cooks to dress them; the expenses of singing men and singing women; the flute, the harp, the
sackbut, and all kinds of music; the dress of the Persian Court how
magnificent! their slaves how numerous! their chariots, their homes,
their pictures, their furniture, what immense sums they had devour-
ed! what expectations from strangers of condition! what exactions!
How shall the youth make his father comprehend that he was cheated at Damascus by one of the best men in the world; that he had
lent a part of his substance to a friend at Nineveh, who had fled off
with it to the Ganges; that a whore of Babylon had swallowed his
best pearl, and anointed the whole city with his balm of Gilead; that
he had been sold by a man of honour for twenty shekels of silver to
a worker in graven images; that the images he had purchased produced him nothing, that they could not be transported across the
wilderness, and had been burnt with fire at Shusan; that the apes
and peacocks which he had sent for from Tharsis lay dead upon his

5*

hands; that the mummies had not been dead long enough which he
had brought from Egypt; that all had gone wrong from the day he
forsook his father's house?"

All this, it must be admitted, is pretty lively for a sermon. But hear the reverend gentleman once more, in the
same discourse, and observe the characteristic coolness
with which he touches, only to drop, what may be called
the "professional" moral of the parable, and glides off
into a train of interesting, but thoroughly mundane, reflections, suggested—or rather, supposed in courtesy to have
been suggested—by the text. "I know not," he says,
"whether it would be a subject of much edification to con-
vince you here that our Saviour, by the Prodigal Son, particularly pointed out those who were sinners of the Gen-
tiles, and were recovered by divine grace to repentance;
and that by the elder brother he intended manifestly the
more froward of the Jews," &c. But, whether it would
edify you or not, he goes on, in effect, to say, I do not
propose to provide you with edification in that kind.
"These uses have been so ably set forth in so many good
sermons upon the Prodigal Son that I shall turn aside
from them at present, and content myself with some reflections upon that fatal passion which led him—and so
many thousands after the example—to gather all he had
together and take his journey into a far country." In
other words, "I propose to make the parable a peg whereon
to hang a few observations on (what does the reader suppose?) the practice of sending young men upon the Grand
Tour, accompanied by a 'bear-leader,' and herein of the
various kinds of bear-leaders, and the services which they
do, and do not, render to their charges; with a few words
on society in Continental cities, and a true view of 'letters
of introduction.'" That is literally the substance of the

remainder of the sermon.   And thus pleasantly does the
preacher play with his curious subject :

"But you will send an able pilot with your son—a scholar.   If
wisdom can speak in no other tongue but Greek or Latin, you do
well; or if mathematics will make a man a gentleman, or natural
philosophy but teach him to make a bow, he may be of some service
in introducing your son into good societies, and supporting him in
them when he had done.   But the upshot will be generally this, that
on the most pressing occasions of addresses, if he is not a mere man
of reading, the unhappy youth will have the tutor to carry, and not
the tutor to carry him.   But (let us say) you will avoid this extreme ;
he shall be escorted by one who knows the world, not only from
books but from his own experience; a man who has been employed
on such services, and thrice ' made the tour of Europe with success '
—that is, without breaking his own or his pupil's neck ; for if he is
such as my eyes have seen, some broken Swiss *valet de chambre*, some
general undertaker, who will perform the journey in so many months,
' if God permit,' much knowledge will not accrue.   Some profit, at
least: he will learn the amount to a halfpenny of every stage from
Calais to Rome; he will be carried to the best inns, instructed where
there is the best wine, and sup a livre cheaper than if the youth had
been left to make the tour and the bargain himself.   Look at our
governor, I beseech you !   See, he is an inch taller as he relates the
advantages.   And here endeth his pride, his knowledge, and his use.
But when your son gets abroad he will be taken out of his hand by
his society with men of rank and letters, with whom he will pass the
greatest part of his time."

So much for the bear-leader ; and now a remark or two
on the young man's chances of getting into good foreign
society ; and then—the benediction :

"Let me observe, in the first place, that company which is really
good is very rare and very shy.   But you have surmounted this difficulty, and procured him the best letters of recommendation to the
most eminent and respectable in every capital.   And I answer that
he will obtain all by them which courtesy strictly stands obliged to

pay on such occasions, but no more. There is nothing in which we
are so much deceived as in the advantages proposed from our con-
nexions and discourse with the literati, &c., in foreign parts, especially if the experiment is made before we are matured by years or
study. Conversation is a traffic; and if you enter it without some
stock of knowledge to balance the account perpetually betwixt you,
the trade drops at once; and this is the reason, however it may be
boasted to the contrary, why travellers have so little (especially good)
conversation with the natives, owing to their suspicion, or perhaps
conviction, that there is nothing to be extracted from the conversation of young itinerants worth the trouble of their bad language, or
the interruption of their visits."

Very true, no doubt, and excellently well put; but we
seem to have got some distance, in spirit at any rate, from
Luke xv. 13; and it is with somewhat too visible effect,
perhaps, that Sterne forces his way back into the orthodox routes of pulpit disquisition. The youth, disappointed with his reception by "the literati," &c., seeks "an
easier society; and as bad company is always ready, and
ever lying in wait, the career is soon finished, and the
poor prodigal returns—the same object of pity with the
prodigal in the Gospel." Hardly a good enough "tag,"
perhaps, to reconcile the ear to the "And now to," &c.,
as a fitting close to this pointed little essay in the style of
the Chesterfield Letters. There is much internal evidence
to show that this so-called sermon was written either after
Sterne's visit to or during his stay in France; and there
is strong reason, I think, to suppose that it was in reality
neither intended for a sermon nor actually delivered from
the pulpit.

No other of his sermons has quite so much vivacity as
this. But in the famous discourse upon an unlucky text
—the sermon preached at the chapel of the English Embassy, in Paris—there are touches of unclerical raillery not

a few. Thus: "What a noise," he exclaims, "among the simulants of the various virtues! . . . Behold Humility, become so out of mere pride; Chastity, never once in harm's way; and Courage, like a Spanish soldier upon an Italian stage—a bladder full of wind. Hush! the sound of that trumpet! Let not my soldier run!' tis some good Christian giving alms. O Pity, thou gentlest of human passions! soft and tender are thy notes, and ill accord they with so loud an instrument."

Here, again, is a somewhat bold saying for a divine: "But, to avoid all commonplace cant as much as I can on this head, I will forbear to say, because I do not think, that 'tis a breach of Christian charity to think or speak ill of our neighbour. We cannot avoid it: our opinion must follow the evidence," &c. And a little later on, commenting on the insinuation conveyed in Satan's question, "Does Job serve God for nought?" he says: "It is a bad picture, and done by a terrible master; and yet we are always copying it. Does a man from real conviction of heart forsake his vices? The position is not to be allowed. No; his vices have forsaken him. Does a pure virgin fear God, and say her prayers? She is in her climacteric? Does humility clothe and educate the unknown orphan? Poverty, thou hast no genealogies. See! is he not the father of the child?" In another sermon he launches out into quaintly contemptuous criticism of a religious movement which he was certainly the last person in the world to understand—to wit, Methodism. He asks whether, "when a poor, disconsolated, drooping creature is terrified from all enjoyment, prays without ceasing till his imagination is heated, fasts and mortifies and mopes till his body is in as bad a plight as his mind, it is a wonder that the mechanical disturbances and conflicts of an empty belly, interpreted by an empty head, should be mistook for workings of a different kind from what they are?" Other sermons reflect the singularly bitter anti-Catholic feeling which was characteristic even of indifferentism in those days—at any rate amongst Whig divines. But in most of them one is liable to come at any moment across one of those strange sallies to which Gray alluded, when he said of the effect of Sterne's sermons upon a reader that "you often see him tottering on the verge of laughter, and ready to throw his periwig in the face of the audience."

CHAPTER VII.

FRANCE AND ITALY.—MEETING WITH WIFE AND DAUGHTER.
—RETURN TO ENGLAND.—"TRISTRAM SHANDY," VOL. IX.
—"THE SENTIMENTAL JOURNEY."

(1765–1768.)

In the first week of October, 1765, or a few days later,
Sterne set out on what was afterwards to become famous
as the "Sentimental Journey through France and Italy."
Not, of course, that all the materials for that celebrated
piece of literary travel were collected on this occasion.
From London as far as Lyons his way lay by a route
which he had already traversed three years before, and
there is reason to believe that at least some of the scenes
in the *Sentimental Journey* were drawn from observation
made on his former visit. His stay in Paris was shorter
this year than it had been on the previous occasion. A
month after leaving England he was at Pont Beauvoisin,
and by the middle of November he had reached Turin.
From this city he writes, with his characteristic simplicity: "I am very happy, and have found my way into a
dozen houses already. To-morrow I am to be presented
to the King, and when that ceremony is over I shall have
my hands full of engagements." From Turin he went on,
by way of Milan, Parma, Piacenza, and Bologna, to Florence, where, after three days' stay, "to dine with our
Plenipo.," he continued his journey to Rome. Here, and

at Naples, he passed the winter of 1765–'66,[1] and prolonged his stay in Italy until the ensuing spring was well
advanced. In the month of May he was again on his way
home, through France, and had had a meeting, after two
years' separation from them, with his wife and daughter.
His account of it to Hall Stevenson is curious: "Never
man," he writes, "has been such a wild-goose chase after
his wife as I have been. After having sought her in five or
six different towns, I found her at last in Franche Comté.
Poor woman!" he adds, "she was very cordial, &c." The
&c. is charming. But her cordiality had evidently no tendency to deepen into any more impassioned sentiment, for
she "begged to stay another year or so." As to "my
Lydia"—the real cause, we must suspect, of Sterne's having turned out of his road—she, he says, "pleases me much.
I found her greatly improved in everything I wished her."
As to himself: "I am most unaccountably well, and most
accountably nonsensical. 'Tis at least a proof of good
spirits, which is a sign and token, in these latter days, that
I must take up my pen. In faith, I think I shall die with
it in my hand; but I shall live these ten years, my Antony,
notwithstanding the fears of my wife, whom I left most
melancholy on that account." The "fears" and the melancholy were, alas! to be justified, rather than the "good
spirits;" and the shears of Atropos were to close, not in
ten years, but in little more than twenty months, upon
that fragile thread of life.

[1] It was on this tour that Sterne picked up the French valet Lafleur, whom he introduced as a character into the *Sentimental Journey*, but whose subsequently published recollections of the tour (if,
indeed, the veritable Lafleur was the author of the notes from which
Scott quotes so freely) appear, as Mr. Fitzgerald has pointed out,
from internal evidence to be mostly fictitious.

By the end of June he was back again in his Yorkshire
home, and very soon after had settled down to work upon
the ninth and last volume of *Tristram Shandy*. He was
writing, however, as it should seem, under something more
than the usual distractions of a man with two establish-
ments. Mrs. Sterne was just then ill at Marseilles, and her
husband—who, to do him justice, was always properly so-
licitous for her material comfort—was busy making pro-
vision for her to change her quarters to Chalons. He
writes to M. Panchaud, at Paris, sending fifty pounds, and
begging him to make her all further advances that might
be necessary. " I have," he says, " such entire confidence
in my wife that she spends as little as she can, though she
is confined to no particular sum . . . and you may rely—
in case she should draw for fifty or a hundred pounds extraordinary—that it and every demand shall be punctually
paid, and with proper thanks; and for this the whole
Shandian family are ready to stand security." Later on,
too, he writes that " a young nobleman is now inaugurat-
ing a jaunt with me for six weeks, about Christmas, to the
Faubourg St. Germain;" and he adds—in a tone the sincerity of which he would himself have probably found a
difficulty in gauging—" if my wife should grow worse
(having had a very poor account of her in my daughter's
last), I cannot think of her being without me; and, however expensive the journey would be, I would fly to Avignon to administer consolation to her and my poor girl."[1]

---

[1] There can be few admirers of Sterne's genius who would not
gladly incline, whenever they find it possible, to Mr. Fitzgerald's very
indulgent estimate of his disposition. But this is only one of many
instances in which the charity of the biographer appears to me to
be, if the expression may be permitted, unconscionable. I can, at
any rate, find no warrant whatever in the above passage for the too

H   8

The necessity for this flight, however, did not arise. Better accounts of Mrs. Sterne arrived a few weeks later, and the husband's consolations were not required.

Meanwhile the idyll of Captain Shandy's love-making was gradually approaching completion; and there are signs to be met with—in the author's correspondence, that is to say, and not in the work itself—that he was somewhat impatient to be done with it, at any rate for the time. " I shall publish," he says, " late in this year; and the next I shall begin a new work of four volumes, which, when finished, I shall continue *Tristram* with fresh spirit." The new work in four volumes (not destined to get beyond one) was, of course, the *Sentimental Journey.* His ninth volume of *Tristram Shandy* was finished by the end of the year, and at Christmas he came up to London, after his usual practice, to see to its publication and enjoy the honours of its reception. The book passed duly through the press, and in the last days of January was issued the announcement of its immediate appearance. Of the character of its welcome I can find no other evidence than that of Sterne himself, in a letter addressed to M. Panchaud some fortnight after the book appeared. " 'Tis liked the best of all here ;" but, with whatever accuracy this may have expressed the complimentary opinion of friends, or even the well-considered judgment of critics, one can hardly believe that it enjoyed anything like the vogue of the former volumes. Sterne, however, would be the less concerned for this, that his head was at the moment full of his new venture. " I am going," he

kindly suggestion that "Sterne was actually negotiating a journey to Paris as ' bear-leader ' to a young nobleman (an odious office, to which he had special aversion), *in order* that he might with economy fly over to Avignon."

writes, " to publish *A Sentimental Journey through France
and Italy*. The undertaking is protected and highly en-
couraged by all our noblesse. 'Tis subscribed for at a
great rate ; 'twill be an original, in large quarto, the subscription half a guinea. If you (Panchaud) can procure
me the honour of a few names of men of science or
fashion, I shall thank you : they will appear in good company, as all the nobility here have honoured me with their
names." As was usual with him, however, he postponed
commencing it until he should have returned to Coxwold ;
and, as was equally usual with him, he found it difficult to
tear himself away from the delights of London. Moreover, there was in the present instance a special difficulty,
arising out of an affair upon which, as it has relations with
the history of Sterne's literary work, it would be impossible, even in the most strictly critical and least general of
biographies, to observe complete silence. I refer, of course,
to the famous and furious flirtation with Mrs. Draper—
the Eliza of the Yorick and Eliza Letters. Of the affair
itself but little need be said. I have already stated my
own views on the general subject of Sterne's love affairs ;
and I feel no inducement to discuss the question of their
innocence or otherwise in relation to this particular amou-
rette. I will only say that were it technically as innocent as
you please, the mean which must be found between Thackeray's somewhat too harsh and Mr. Fitzgerald's considerably too indulgent judgment on it will lie, it seems to me,
decidedly nearer to the former than to the latter's extreme.
This episode of violently sentimental philandering with an
Indian "grass widow" was, in any case, an extremely un-
lovely passage in Sterne's life. On the best and most
charitable view of it, the flirtation, pursued in the way it
was, and to the lengths to which it was carried, must be

held to convict the elderly lover of the most deplorable
levity, vanity, indiscretion, and sickly sentimentalism. It
was, to say the least of it, most unbecoming in a man of
Sterne's age and profession; and when it is added that
Yorick's attentions to Eliza were paid in so open a fashion
as to be brought by gossip to the ears of his neglected
wife, then living many hundred miles away from him, its
highly reprehensible character seems manifest enough in
all ways.

No sooner, however, had the fascinating widow set sail,
than the sentimental lover began to feel so strongly the
need of a female consoler, that his heart seems to have
softened, insensibly, even towards his wife. " I am unhappy," he writes plaintively to Lydia Sterne. " Thy
mother and thyself at a distance from me—and what can
compensate for such a destitution? For God's sake persuade her to come and fix in England! for life is too
short to waste in separation; and while she lives in one
country and I in another, many people will suppose it
proceeds from choice"—a supposition, he seems to imply,
which even my scrupulously discreet conduct in her absence
scarcely suffices to refute. " Besides "—a word in which
there is here almost as much virtue as in an" if "—" I want
thee near me, thou child and darling of my heart. I am
in a melancholy mood, and my Lydia's eyes will smart
with weeping when I tell her the cause that just now
affects me." And then his sensibilities brim over, and
into his daughter's ear he pours forth his lamentations
over the loss of her mother's rival. " I am apprehensive
the dear friend I mentioned in my last letter is going into
a decline. I was with her two days ago, and I never be-
held a being so altered. She has a tender frame, and looks
like a drooping lily, for the roses are fled from her cheeks.

I can never see or talk to this incomparable woman without bursting into tears. I have a thousand obligations to
her, and I love her more than her whole sex, if not all the
world put together. She has a delicacy," &c., &c. And
after reciting a frigid epitaph which he had written, " ex-
pressive of her modest worth," he winds up with—" Say
all that is kind of me to thy mother; and believe me, my
Lydia, that I love thee most truly." My excuse for quoting thus fully from this most characteristic letter, and, indeed, for dwelling at all upon these closing incidents of the
Yorick and Eliza episode, is, that in their striking illus-
tion of the soft, weak, spiritually self-indulgent nature
of the man, they assist us, far more than many pages
of criticism would do, to understand one particular aspect
of his literary idiosyncrasy. The sentimentalist of real life
explains the sentimentalist in art.

In the early days of May Sterne managed at last to tear
himself away from London and its joys, and with painful
slowness, for he was now in a wretched state of health, to
make his way back to Yorkshire. " I have got conveyed,"
he says in a distressing letter from Newark to Hall Stevenson—" I have got conveyed thus far like a bale of cadav-
erous goods consigned to Pluto and Company, lying in the
bottom of my chaise most of the route, upon a large pillow
which I had the *prévoyance* to purchase before I set out.
I am worn out, but pass on to Barnby Moor to-night, and
if possible to York the next. I know not what is the
matter with me, but some derangement presses hard upon
this machine. Still, I think it will not be overset this
bout"—another of those utterances of a cheerful courage
under the prostration of pain which reveal to us the man-
liest side of Sterne's nature. On reaching Coxwold his
health appears to have temporarily mended, and in June

we find him giving a far better account of himself to another of his friends. The fresh Yorkshire air seems to
have temporarily revived him, and to his friend, Arthur
Lee, a young American, he writes thus: " I am as happy
as a prince at Coxwold, and I wish you could see in how
princely a manner I live. 'Tis a land of plenty. I sit
down alone to dinner—fish and wild-fowl, or a couple of
fowls or ducks, with cream and all the simple plenty which
a rich valley under Hamilton Hills can produce, with a
clean cloth on my table, and a bottle of wine on my right
hand to drink your health. I have a hundred hens and
chickens about my yard; and not a parishioner catches a
hare, a rabbit, or a trout but he brings it as an offering to
me." Another of his correspondents at this period was
the Mrs. H. of his letters, whose identity I have been unable to trace, but who is addressed in a manner which
seems to show Sterne's anxiety to expel the old flame of
Eliza's kindling by a new one. There is little, indeed, of
the sentimentalizing strain in which he was wont to sigh
at the feet of Mrs. Draper, but in its place there is a freedom of a very prominent, and here and there of a highly
unpleasant, kind. To his friends, Mr. and Mrs. James, too,
he writes frequently during this year, chiefly to pour out
his soul on the subject of Eliza; and Mrs. James, who is
always addressed in company with her husband, enjoys
the almost unique distinction of being the only woman
outside his own family circle whom Sterne never approaches in the language of artificial gallantry, but always
in that of simple friendship and respect.[1] Meanwhile,

[1] To this period of Sterne's life, it may here be remarked, is to
be assigned the dog-Latin letter ("and very sad dog-Latin too") so
justly animadverted upon by Thackeray, and containing a passage
of which Madame de Medalle, it is to be charitably hoped, had no

however, the *Sentimental Journey* was advancing at a reasonable rate of speed towards completion. In July he writes of himself as "now beginning to be truly busy" on it, "the pain and sorrows of this life having retarded its progress."

His wife and daughter were about to rejoin him in the autumn, and he looked forward to settling them at a hired house in York before going up to town to publish his new volumes. On the 1st of October the two ladies arrived at York, and the next day the reunited family went on to Coxwold. The meeting with the daughter gave Sterne one of the few quite innocent pleasures which he was capable of feeling; and he writes next day to Mr. and Mrs. James in terms of high pride and satisfaction of his recovered child. "My girl has returned," he writes, in the language of playful affection, "an elegant, accomplished little slut. My wife — but I hate," he adds, with remarkable presence of mind, "to praise my wife. 'Tis as much as decency will allow to praise my daughter. I suppose," he concludes, "they will return next summer to France. They leave me in a month to reside at York for the winter, and I stay at Coxwold till the 1st of January." This seems to indicate a little longer delay in the publication of the *Sentimental Journey* than he had at first intended; for it seems that the book was finished by the end of November. On

suspicion of the meaning. Mr. Fitzgerald, through an oversight in translation, and understanding Sterne to say that he himself, and not his correspondent, Hall Stevenson, was "quadraginta et plus annos natus," has referred it to an earlier date. The point, however, is of no great importance, as the untranslatable passage in the letter would be little less unseemly in 1754 or 1755 than in 1768, at the beginning of which year, since the letter is addressed from London to Hall Stevenson, then in Yorkshire, it must, in fact, have been written.

the 28th of that month he writes to the Earl of —— (as his daughter's foolish mysteriousness has headed the letter), to thank him for his letter of inquiry about Yorick, and to say that Yorick "has worn out both his spirits and body with the *Sentimental Journey.* 'Tis true that an author must feel himself, or his reader will not" (how mistaken a devotion Sterne showed to this Horatian canon will be noted hereafter), "but I have torn my whole frame into pieces by my feelings. I believe the brain stands as much in need of recruiting as the body; therefore I shall set out for town the 20th of next month, after having recruited myself at York." Then he adds the strange observation, "I might, indeed, solace myself with my wife (who is come from France), but, in fact, I have long been a sentimental being, whatever your Lordship may think to the contrary. The world has imagined because I wrote *Tristram Shandy* that I was myself more Shandian than I really ever was. 'Tis a good-natured world we live in, and we are often painted in divers colours, according to the ideas each one frames in his head." It would, perhaps, have been scarcely possible for Sterne to state his essentially unhealthy philosophy of life so concisely as in this naïve passage. The connubial affections are here, in all seriousness and good faith apparently, opposed to the sentimental emotions—as the lower to the higher. To indulge the former is to be "Shandian," that is to say, coarse and carnal; to devote oneself to the latter, or, in other words, to spend one's days in semi-erotic languishings over the whole female sex indiscriminately, is to show spirituality and taste.

Meanwhile, however, that fragile abode of sentimentalism—that frame which had just been "torn to pieces" by the feelings — was becoming weaker than its owner supposed. Much of the exhaustion which Sterne had attributed to the violence of his literary emotions was no doubt due to the rapid decline of bodily powers which, unknown to him, were already within a few months of their final collapse. He did not set out for London on the 20th of December, as he had promised himself, for on that day he was only just recovering from "an attack of fever and bleeding at the lungs," which had confined him to his room for nearly three weeks. "I am worn down to a shadow," he writes on the 23rd, "but as my fever has left me, I set off the latter end of next week with my friend, Mr. Hall, for town." His home affairs had already been settled. Early in December it had been arranged that his wife and daughter should only remain at York during the winter, and should return to the Continent in the spring. "Mrs. Sterne's health," he writes, "is insupportable in England. She must return to France, and justice and humanity forbid me to oppose it." But separation from his wife meant separation from his daughter; it was this, of course, which was the really painful parting, and it is to the credit of Sterne's disinterestedness of affection for Lydia, that in his then state of health he brought himself to consent to her leaving him. But he recognized that it was for the advantage of her prospect of settling herself in life that she should go with her mother, who seemed "inclined to establish her in France, where she has had many advantageous offers." Nevertheless "his heart bled," as he wrote to Lee, when he thought of parting with his child. "'Twill be like the separation of soul and body, and equal to nothing but what passes at that tremendous moment; and like it in one respect, for she will be in one kingdom while I am in another." Thus was this matter settled, and by the 1st of January Sterne

6

had arrived in London for the last time, with the two
volumes of the *Sentimental Journey*. He took up his
quarters at the lodgings in Bond Street (No. 41), which
he had occupied during his stay in town the previous year,
and entered at once upon the arrangements for publication.
These occupied two full months, and on the 27th of February the last work, as it was destined to be, of the Rev.
Mr. Yorick was issued to the world.

Its success would seem to have been immediate, and was
certainly great and lasting. In one sense, indeed, it was
far greater than had been, or than has since been, attained
by *Tristram Shandy*. The compliments which courteous
Frenchmen had paid the author upon his former work, and
which his simple vanity had swallowed whole and unsea-
soned, without the much-needed grain of salt, might, no
doubt, have been repeated to him with far greater sincerity as regards the *Sentimental Journey*, had he lived to
receive them. Had any Frenchman told him a year or
two afterwards that the latter work was " almost as much
known in Paris as in London, at least among men of condition and learning," he would very likely have been telling him no more than the truth. The *Sentimental Journey* certainly acquired what *Tristram Shandy* never did
—a European reputation. It has been translated into
Italian, German, Dutch, and even Polish ; and into French
again and again. The French, indeed, have no doubt whatever of its being Sterne's *chef-d'œuvre* ; and one has only
to compare a French translation of it with a rendering of
Tristram Shandy into the same language to understand,
and from our neighbours' point of view even to admit, the
justice of their preference. The charms of the *Journey*,
its grace, wit, and urbanity, are thoroughly congenial to
that most graceful of languages, and reproduce themselves

readily enough therein; while, on the other hand, the fan-
tastic digressions, the elaborate mystifications, the farcical
interludes of the earlier work, appear intolerably awkward
and *bizzare* in their French dress; and, what is much more
strange, even the point of the *double entendres* is sometimes
unaccountably lost. Were it not that the genuine humour
of *Tristram Shandy* in a great measure evaporates in translation, one would be forced to admit that the work which
is the more catholic in its appeal to appreciation is the better of the two. But, having regard to this disappearance
of genuine and unquestionable excellences in the process
of translation, I see no good reason why those Englishmen
—the great majority, I imagine — who prefer *Tristram
Shandy* to the *Sentimental Journey* should feel any mis-
givings as to the soundness of their taste. The humour
which goes the deepest down beneath the surface of things
is the most likely to become inextricably interwoven with
those deeper fibres of associations which lie at the roots
of a language; and it may well happen, therefore, though
from the cosmopolitan point of view it is a melancholy
reflection, that the merit of a book, to those who use the
language in which it is written, bears a direct ratio to the
persistence of its refusal to yield up its charm to men of
another tongue.

The favour, however, with which the *Sentimental Journey* was received abroad, and which it still enjoys (the last
French translation is very recent), is, as Mr. Fitzgerald says,
" worthily merited, if grace, nature, true sentiment, and exquisite dramatic power be qualities that are to find a welcome. And apart," he · adds, " from these attractions it
has a unique charm of its own, a flavour, so to speak, a
fragrance that belongs to that one book alone. Never
was there such a charming series of complete little pict-

ures, which for delicacy seem like the series of medallions
done on Sèvres china which we sometimes see in old
French cabinets. . . . The figures stand out brightly, and
in what number and variety! Old Calais, with its old
inn; M. Dessein, the monk, one of the most artistic figures on literary canvas; the charming French lady whom
M. Dessein shut into the carriage with the traveller; the
débonnaire French captain, and the English travellers returning, touched in with only a couple of strokes; La
Fleur, the valet; the pretty French glove-seller, whose
pulse the Sentimental one felt; her husband, who passed
through the shop and pulled off his hat to Monsieur for
the honour he was doing him; the little maid in the bookseller's shop, who put her little present *à part;* the charming Greuze 'grisset,' who sold him the ruffles; the reduced
chevalier selling *patés;* the groups of beggars at Montreuil;
the *fade* Count de Bissie, who read Shakspeare; and the
crowd of minor *croquis*—postilions, landlords, notaries, soldiers, abbés, *précieuses*, maids—merely touched, but touched with wonderful art, make up a surprising collection of
distinct and graphic characters."

CHAPTER VIII.

LAST DAYS AND DEATH.

(1768.)

THE end was now fast approaching. Months before, Sterne had written doubtfully of his being able to stand another winter in England, and his doubts were to be fatally justified. One can easily see, however, how the unhappy experiment came to be tried. It is possible that he might have delayed the publication of his book for a while, and taken refuge abroad from the rigours of the two remaining winter months, had it not been in the nature of his malady to conceal its deadly approaches. Consumption sported with its victim in the cruel fashion that is its wont. "I continue to mend," Sterne writes from Bond Street on the first day of the new year, "and doubt not but this with all other evils and uncertainties of life will end for the best." And for the best perhaps it did end, in the sense in which the resigned Christian uses these pious words; but this, one fears, was not the sense intended by the dying man. All through January and February he was occupied not only with business, but as it would seem with a fair amount, though less, no doubt, than his usual share, of pleasure also. Vastly active was he, it seems, in the great undertaking of obtaining tickets for one of Mrs. Cornely's entertainments —the "thing" to go to at that particular time—for his friends the Jameses. He writes them on Monday that he has not been a moment at rest since writing the previous day about the Soho ticket. "I have been at a Secretary of State to get one, have been upon one knee to my friend Sir George Macartney, Mr. Lascelles, and Mr. Fitzmaurice, without mentioning five more. I believe I could as soon get you a place at Court, for everybody is going; but I will go out and try a new circle, and if you do not hear from me by a quarter to three, you may conclude I have been unfortunate in my supplications." Whether he was or was not unfortunate history does not record. A week or two later the old round of dissipation had apparently set in. "I am now tied down neck and heels by engagements every night this week, or most joyfully would have trod the old pleasing road from Bond to Gerrard Street. . . . . I am quite well, but exhausted with a roomful of company every morning till dinner." A little later, and this momentary flash of health had died out; and we find him writing what was his last letter to his daughter, full, evidently, of uneasy forebodings as to his approaching end. He speaks of "this vile influenza—be not alarmed. I think I shall get the better of it, and shall be with you both the 1st of May;" though, he adds, "if I escape, 'twill not be for a long period, my child — unless a quiet retreat and peace of mind can restore me." But the occasion of this letter was a curious one, and a little more must be extracted from it. Lydia Sterne's letter to her father had, he said, astonished him. "She (Mrs. Sterne) could know but little of my feelings to tell thee that under the supposition I should survive thy mother I should bequeath thee as a legacy to Mrs. Draper. No, my Lydia, 'tis a lady whose virtues I wish thee to imitate"—Mrs. James, in fact, whom he proceeds to praise with much and probably well-deserved warmth. "But," he adds, sadly, "I think, my Lydia, thy mother will survive me; do not deject her spirit with thy apprehensions on my account. I have sent you a necklace and buckles, and the same to your mother. My girl cannot form a wish that is in the power of her father that he will not gratify her in; and I cannot in justice be less kind to thy mother. I am never alone. The kindness of my friends is ever the same. I wish though I had thee to nurse me, but I am denied that. Write to me twice a week at least. God bless thee, my child, and believe me ever, ever, thy affectionate father." The despondent tone of this letter was to be only too soon justified. The "vile influenza" proved to be or became a pleurisy. On Thursday, March 10, he was bled three times, and blistered on the day after. And on the Tuesday following, in evident consciousness that his end was near, he penned that cry "for pity and pardon," as Thackeray calls it—the first as well as the last, and which sounds almost as strange as it does piteous from those mocking lips:

"The physician says I am better. . . . God knows, for I feel myself sadly wrong, and shall, if I recover, be a long while of gaining strength. Before I have gone through half the letter I must stop to rest my weak hand a dozen times. Mr. James was so good as to call upon me yesterday. I felt emotions not to be described at the sight of him, and he overjoyed me by talking a great deal of you. Do, dear Mrs. James, entreat him to come to-morrow or next day, for perhaps I have not many days or hours to live. I want to ask a favour of him, if I find myself worse, that I shall beg of you if in this wrestling I come off conqueror. My spirits are fled. It is a bad omen; do not weep, my dear lady. Your tears are too precious to be shed for me. Bottle them up, and may the cork never be drawn. Dearest, kindest, gentlest, and best of women! may health, peace, and happiness prove your handmaids. If I die, cherish the remembrance of

me, and forget the follies which you so often condemned, which my
heart, not my head, betrayed me into. Should my child, my Lydia,
want a mother, may I hope you will (if she is left parentless) take her
to your bosom? You are the only woman on earth I can depend
upon for such a benevolent action. I wrote to her a fortnight ago,
and told her what, I trust, she will find in you. Mr. James will be a
father to her. . . . Commend me to him, as I now commend you to
that Being who takes under his care the good and kind part of the
world. Adieu, all grateful thanks to you and Mr. James.

"From your affectionate friend,   L. STERNE."

This pathetic death-bed letter is superscribed "Tuesday." It seems to have been written on Tuesday, the 15th
of March, and three days later the writer breathed his last.
But two persons, strangers both, were present at his death-
bed, and it is by a singularly fortunate chance, therefore,
that one of these—and he not belonging to the class of
people who usually leave behind them published records
of the events of their lives—should have preserved for us
an account of the closing scene. This, however, is to be
found in the Memoirs of John Macdonald, "a cadet of the
house of Keppoch," at that time footman to Mr. Crawford,
a fashionable friend of Sterne's. His master had taken a
house in Clifford Street in the spring of 1768; and "about
this time," he writes, "Mr. Sterne, the celebrated author,
was taken ill at the silk-bag shop in Old Bond Street.
He was sometimes called Tristram Shandy and sometimes
Yorick, a very great favourite of the gentlemen. One
day"—namely, on the aforesaid 18th of March—"my
master had company to dinner who were speaking about
him—the Duke of Roxburghe, the Earl of March, the Earl
of Ossory, the Duke of Grafton, Mr. Garrick, Mr. Hume,
and a Mr. James." Many, if not most, of the party, therefore, were personal friends of the man who lay dying in
the street hard by, and naturally enough the conversation

turned on his condition. "'John,'" said my master," the narrative continues, "'go and inquire how Mr. Sterne is to-day.'" Macdonald did so; and, in language which seems to bear the stamp of truth upon it, he thus records the grim story which he had to report to the assembled guests on his return: "I went to Mr. Sterne's lodgings; the mistress opened the door. I enquired how he did; she told me to go up to the nurse. I went into the room, and he was just a-dying. I waited ten minutes; but in five he said, 'Now it is come.' He put up his hand as if to stop a blow, and died in a minute. The gentlemen were all very sorry, and lamented him very much."

Thus, supported by a hired nurse, and under the curious eyes of a stranger, Sterne breathed his last. His wife and daughter were far away; the convivial associates " who were all very sorry and lamented him very much," were for the moment represented only by "John ;" and the shocking tradition goes that the alien hands by which the " dying eyes were closed," and the " decent limbs composed," remunerated themselves for the pious office by abstracting the gold sleeve-links from the dead man's wrists. One may hope, indeed, that this last circumstance is to be rejected as sensational legend, but even without it the story of Sterne's death seems sad enough, no doubt. Yet it is, after all, only by contrast with the excited gaiety of his daily life in London that his end appears so forlorn. From many a "set of residential chambers," from many of the old and silent inns of the lawyers, departures as lonely, or lonelier, are being made around us in London every year: the departures of men not necessarily kinless or friendless, but living solitary lives, and dying before their friends or kindred can be summoned to their bedsides. Such deaths, no doubt, are often contrasted in conventional pathos with that of the husband and father surrounded by a weeping wife and children ; but the more sensible among us construct no tragedy out of a mode of exit which must have many times entered as at least a possibility into the previous contemplation of the dying man. And except, as has been said, that Sterne associates himself in our minds with the perpetual excitements of lively companionship, there would be nothing particularly melancholy in his end. This is subject, of course, to the assumption that the story of his landlady having stolen the gold sleeve-links from his dead body may be treated as mythical; and, rejecting this story, there seems no good reason for making much ado about the manner of his death. Of friends, as distinguished from mere dinner-table acquaintances, he seems to have had but few in London : with the exception of the Jameses, one knows not with certainty of any ; and the Jameses do not appear to have neglected him in the illness which neither they nor he suspected to be his last. Mr. James had paid him a visit but a day or two before the end came ; and it may very likely have been upon his report of his friend's condition that the message of inquiry was sent from the dinner table at which he was a guest. No doubt Sterne's flourish in *Tristram Shandy* about his preferring to die at an inn, untroubled by the spectacle of "the concern of my friends, and the last services of wiping my brows and smoothing my pillow," was a mere piece of bravado ; and the more probably so because the reflection is appropriated almost bodily from Bishop Burnet, who quotes it as a frequent observation of Archbishop Leighton. But, considering that Sterne was in the habit of passing nearly half of each year alone in London lodgings, the realization of his wish does not strike me, I confess, as so dramatically impressive a coincidence as it is sometimes represented.

According, however, to one strange story the dramatic element gives place after Sterne's very burial to melodrama of the darkest kind. The funeral, which pointed, after all, a far sadder moral than the death, took place on Tuesday, March 22, attended by only two mourners, one of whom is said to have been his publisher Becket, and the other probably Mr. James; and, thus duly neglected by the whole crowd of boon companions, the remains of Yorick were consigned to the " new burying-ground near Tyburn " of the parish of St. George's, Hanover Square. In that now squalid and long-decayed grave-yard, within sight of the Marble Arch and over against the broad expanse of Hyde Park, is still to be found a tombstone inscribed with some inferior lines to the memory of the departed humourist, and with a statement, inaccurate by eight months, of the date of his death, and a year out as to his age. Dying, as has been seen, on the 18th of March, 1768, at the age of fifty-four, he is declared on this slab to have died on the 13th of November, aged fifty-three years. There is more excuse, however, for this want of veracity than sepulchral inscriptions can usually plead. The stone was erected by the pious hands of " two brother Masons," many years, it is said, after the event which it purports to record; and from the wording of the epitaph which commences, " Near this place lyes the body," &c., it obviously does not profess to indicate—what, doubtless, there was no longer any means of tracing—the exact spot in which Sterne's remains were laid. But, wherever the grave really was, the body interred in it, according to the strange story to which I have referred, is no longer there. That story goes: that two days after the burial, on the night of the 24th of March, the corpse was stolen by body-snatchers, and by them disposed of to M. Collignon, Professor of Anatomy at Cambridge; that the Professor invited a few scientific friends to witness a demonstration, and that among these was one who had been acquainted with Sterne, and who fainted with horror on recognizing in the already partially dissected "subject" the features of his friend. So, at least, this very gruesome and Poe-like legend runs; but it must be confessed that all the evidence which Mr. Fitzgerald has been able to collect in its favour is of the very loosest and vaguest description. On the other hand, it is, of course, only fair to recollect that, in days when respectable surgeons and grave scientific professors had to depend upon the assistance of law-breakers for the prosecution of their studies and teachings, every effort would naturally be made to hush up any such unfortunate affair. There is, moreover, independent evidence to the fact that similar desecrations of this grave-yard had of late been very common; and that at least one previous attempt to check the operations of the "resurrection-men" had been attended with peculiarly infelicitous results. In the *St. James's Chronicle* for November 26, 1767, we find it recorded that "the Burying Ground in Oxford Road, belonging to the Parish of St. George's, Hanover Square, having been lately robbed of several dead bodies, a Watcher was placed there, attended by a large mastiff Dog; notwithstanding which, on Sunday night last, some Villains found means to steal out another dead Body, and carried off the very Dog." Body-snatchers so adroit and determined as to contrive to make additional profit out of the actual means taken to prevent their depredations, would certainly not have been deterred by any considerations of prudence from attempting the theft of Sterne's corpse. There was no such ceremony about his funeral as would lead them to suppose that the deceased was a person of any importance, or one whose body could not be stolen without a risk of creating undesirable excitement. On the whole, therefore, it is impossible to reject the body-snatching story as certainly fabulous, though its truth is far from being proved; and though I can scarcely myself subscribe to Mr. Fitzgerald's view, that there is a "grim and lurid Shandyism" about the scene of dissection, yet if others discover an appeal to their sense of humour in the idea of Sterne's body being dissected after death, I see nothing to prevent them from holding that hypothesis as a "pious opinion."

CHAPTER IX.

EVERYDAY experience suffices to show that the qualities
which win enduring fame for books and for their authors
are not always those to which they owe their first popularity. It may with the utmost probability be affirmed
that this was the case with *Tristram Shandy* and with
Sterne. We cannot, it is true, altogether dissociate the
permanent attractions of the novel from those characteristics of it which have long since ceased to attract at all;
the two are united in a greater or less degree throughout
the work; and this being so, it is, of course, impossible to
prove to demonstration that it was the latter qualities, and
not the former, which procured it its immediate vogue.
But, as it happens, it is possible to show that what may
be called its spurious attractions varied directly, and its
real merits inversely, as its popularity with the public of
its day. In the higher qualities of humour, in dramatic
vigour, in skilful and subtle delineation of character, the
novel showed no deterioration, but, in some instances, a
marked improvement, as it proceeded; yet the second instalment was not more popular, and most of the succeeding ones were distinctly less popular, than the first. They
had gained in many qualities, while they had lost in only
the single one of novelty; and we may infer, therefore,

with approximate certainty, that what "took the town" in the first instance was, that quality of the book which was strangest at its first appearance. The mass of the public read, and enjoyed, or thought they enjoyed, when they were really only puzzled and perplexed. The wild digressions, the audacious impertinences, the burlesque philosophizing, the broad jests, the air of recondite learning, all combined to make the book a nine days' wonder; and a majority of its readers would probably have been prepared to pronounce *Tristram Shandy* a work as original in scheme and conception as it was eccentric. Some there were, no doubt, who perceived the influence of Rabelais in the incessant digressions and the burlesque of philosophy; others, it may be, found a reminder of Burton in the parade of learning; and yet a few others, the scattered students of French facetiæ of the fourteenth and fifteenth centuries, may have read the broad jests with a feeling that they had "seen something like it before." But no single reader, no single critic of the time, appears to have combined the knowledge necessary for tracing these three characteristics of the novel to their respective sources; and none certainly had any suspicion of the extent to which the books and authors from whom they were imitated had been laid under contribution. No one suspected that Sterne, not content with borrowing his trick of rambling from Rabelais, and his airs of erudition from Burton, and his fooleries from Bruscambille, had coolly transferred whole passages from the second of these writers, not only without acknowledgment, but with the intention, obviously indicated by his mode of procedure, of passing them off as his own. Nay, it was not till full fifty years afterwards that these daring robberies were detected, or, at any rate, revealed to the world; and, with an irony which Sterne

himself would have appreciated, it was reserved for a sincere admirer of the humourist to play the part of detective. In 1812 Dr. John Ferriar published his *Illustrations
of Sterne,* and the prefatory sonnet, in which he solicits
pardon for his too minute investigations, is sufficient proof
of the curiously reverent spirit in which he set about his
damaging task :

> "Sterne, for whose sake I plod through miry ways
> Of antic wit, and quibbling mazes drear,
> Let not thy shade malignant censure fear,
> If aught of inward mirth my search betrays.
> Long slept that mirth in dust of ancient days,
> Erewhile to Guise or wanton Valois dear," &c.

Thus commences Dr. Ferriar's apology, which, however,
can hardly be held to cover his offence ; for, as a matter
of fact, Sterne's borrowings extend to a good deal besides
"mirth;" and some of the most unscrupulous of these
forced loans are raised from passages of a perfectly serious import in the originals from which they are taken.

Here, however, is the list of authors to whom Dr. Ferriar holds Sterne to have been more or less indebted:
Rabelais, Beroalde de Verville, Bouchet, Bruscambille, Scarron, Swift, an author of the name or pseudonym of "Ga-
briel John," Burton, Bacon, Blount, Montaigne, Bishop Hall.
The catalogue is a reasonably long one; but it is not, of
course, to be supposed that Sterne helped himself equally
freely from every author named in it. His obligations to
some of them are, as Dr. Ferriar admits, but slight. From
Rabelais, besides his vagaries of narrative, Sterne took, no
doubt, the idea of the *Tristra-pœdia* (by descent from the
"education of Pantagruel," through "Martinus Scrible-
rus"); but though he has appropriated bodily the passage
in which Friar John attributes the beauty of his nose to

the pectoral conformation of his nurse, he may be said to
have constructively acknowledged the debt in a reference
to one of the characters in the Rabelaisian dialogue.[1]

Upon Beroalde, again, upon D'Aubigné, and upon Bouchet he has made no direct and *verbatim* depredations.
From Bruscambille he seems to have taken little or nothing but the not very valuable idea of the tedious buffoon-
ery of vol. iii. c. 30, *et sqq.*; and to Scarron he, perhaps,
owed the incident of the dwarf at the theatre in the *Sentimental Journey*, an incident which, it must be owned, he
vastly improved in the taking. All this, however, does not
amount to very much, and it is only when we come to Dr.
Ferriar's collations of *Tristram Shandy* with the *Anatomy
of Melancholy* that we begin to understand what feats
Sterne was capable of as a plagiarist. He must, to begin
with, have relied with cynical confidence on the conviction
that famous writers are talked about and not read, for he
sets to work with the scissors upon Burton's first page:
"Man, the most excellent and noble creature of the world,
the principal and mighty work of God; wonder of nature,
as Zoroaster calls him; *audacis naturæ miraculum*, the
marvel of marvels, as Plato; the abridgment and epitome
of the world, as Pliny," &c. Thus Burton; and, with a

---

[1] "There is no cause but one," said my Uncle Toby, "why one
man's nose is longer than another, but because that God pleases to
have it so." "That is Grangousier's solution," said my father.
"'Tis He," continued my Uncle Toby, "who makes us all, and frames
and puts us together in such forms . . . and for such ends as is
agreeable to His infinite wisdom."—*Tristram Shandy*, vol. iii. c. 41.
"Par ce, repondit Grangousier, qu'ainsi Dieu l'a voulu, lequel nous
fait en cette forme et cette fin selon divin arbitre."—*Rabelais*, book i.
c. 41. In another place, however (vol. viii. c. 3), Sterne has borrowed
a whole passage from this French humourist without any acknowledgment at all.

few additions of his own, and the substitution of Aristotle
for Plato as the author of one of the descriptions, thus
Sterne: "Who made MAN with powers which dart him
from heaven to earth in a moment—that great, that most
excellent and noble creature of the world, the miracle of
nature, as Zoroaster, in his book περὶ φύσεως, called him—
the Shekinah of the Divine Presence, as Chrysostom—the
image of God, as Moses—the ray of Divinity, as Plato—
the marvel of marvels, as Aristotle," &c.[1] And in the
same chapter, in the "Fragment upon Whiskers," Sterne
relates how a "decayed kinsman" of the Lady Baussiere
"ran begging, bareheaded, on one side of her palfrey, conjuring her by the former bonds of friendship, alliance, consanguinity, &c.—cousin, aunt, sister, mother—for virtue's
sake, for your own sake, for mine, for Christ's sake, remember me! pity me!" And again he tells how a "de-
vout, venerable, hoary-headed man" thus beseeched her:
"'I beg for the unfortunate. Good my lady, 'tis for a
prison—for an hospital; 'tis for an old man—a poor man
undone by shipwreck, by suretyship, by fire. I call God
and all His angels to witness, 'tis to clothe the naked, to
feed the hungry—'tis to comfort the sick and the broken-
hearted.' The Lady Baussiere rode on."[2]

But now compare this passage from the *Anatomy of
Melancholy*:

"A poor decayed kinsman of his sets upon him by the way, in all
his jollity, and runs begging, bareheaded, by him, conjuring him by
those former bonds of friendship, alliance, consanguinity, &c., 'uncle,
cousin, brother, father, show some pity for Christ's sake, pity a
sick man, an old man,' &c.; he cares not—ride on: pretend sick-
ness, inevitable loss of limbs, plead suretyship or shipwreck, fire,
common calamities, show thy wants and imperfections, take God

---

[1] *Tristram Shandy*, vol. v. c. 1.   [2] *Ibid.*

and all His angels to witness . . . put up a supplication to him in
the name of a thousand orphans, an hospital, a spittle, a prison, as
he goes by . . . ride on.[1]

Hardly a casual coincidence this. But it is yet more
unpleasant to find that the mock philosophic reflections
with which Mr. Shandy consoles himself on Bobby's
death, in those delightful chapters on that event, are not
taken, as they profess to be, direct from the sages of an-
tiquity, but have been conveyed through, and "conveyed"
from, Burton.

"When Agrippina was told of her son's death," says
Sterne, "Tacitus informs us that, not being able to mod-
erate her passions, she abruptly broke off her work."
Tacitus does, it is true, inform us of this. But it was undoubtedly Burton (*Anat. Mel.*, p. 213) who informed Sterne
of it. So, too, when Mr. Shandy goes on to remark upon
death that "'Tis an inevitable chance—the first statute in
Magna Charta—it is an everlasting Act of Parliament, my
dear brother—all must die," the agreement of his views
with those of Burton, who had himself said of death, "'Tis
an inevitable chance—the first statute in Magna Charta—
an everlasting Act of Parliament—all must die,"[2] is even
textually exact.

In the next passage, however, the humourist gets the
better of the plagiarist, and we are ready to forgive the
theft for the happily comic turn which he gives to it.
Burton:

"Tully was much grieved for his daughter Tulliola's death at first,
until such time that he had confirmed his mind by philosophical pre-
cepts; then he began to triumph over fortune and grief, and for her
reception into heaven to be much more joyed than before he was
troubled for her loss."

---

[1] Burton: *Anat. Mel.*, p. 269.   [2] *Ibid.*, p. 215.

Sterne:

"When Tully was bereft of his daughter, at first he laid it to his
heart, he listened to the voice of nature, and modulated his own unto
it. O my Tullia! my daughter! my child!—Still, still, still—'twas O
my Tullia, my Tullia! Methinks I see my Tullia, I hear my Tullia,
I talk with my Tullia. But as soon as he began to look into the
stores of philosophy, and *consider how many excellent things might be
said upon the occasion*, nobody on earth can conceive, says the great
orator, how happy, how joyful it made me."

"Kingdoms and provinces, cities and towns," continues
Burton, "have their periods, and are consumed." "Kingdoms and provinces, and towns and cities," exclaims Mr.
Shandy, throwing the sentence, like the "born orator"
his son considered him, into the rhetorical interrogative,
"have they not their periods?" "Where," he proceeds,
"is Troy, and Mycenæ, and Thebes, and Delos, and Per-
sepolis, and Agrigentum? What is become, brother Toby,
of Nineveh and Babylon, of Cyzicum and Mytilene? The
fairest towns that ever the sun rose upon" (and all, with
the curious exception of Mytilene, enumerated by Burton)
"are now no more." And then the famous consolatory
letter from Servius Sulpicius to Cicero on the death of
Tullia is laid under contribution—Burton's rendering of
the Latin being followed almost word for word. "Returning out of Asia," declaims Mr. Shandy, "when I sailed
from Ægina towards Megara" (when can this have been?
thought my Uncle Toby), "I began to view the country
round about. Ægina was behind me, Megara before," &c.,
and so on, down to the final reflection of the philosopher,
"Remember that thou art but a man;" at which point
Sterne remarks coolly, "Now, my Uncle Toby knew not
that this last paragraph was an extract of Servius Sulpicius's consolatory letter to Tully"—the thing to be really

known being that the paragraph was, in fact, Servius Sulpicius filtered through Burton. Again, and still quoting
from the *Anatomy of Melancholy*, Mr. Shandy remarks
how "the Thracians wept when a child was born, and
feasted and made merry when a man went out of the
world; and with reason." He then goes on to lay pred-
atory hands on that fine, sad passage in Lucian, which
Burton had quoted before him : " Is it not better not to
hunger at all, than to eat ? not to thirst, than to take physic
to cure it ?" (why not " than to drink to satisfy thirst ?"
as Lucian wrote and Burton translated). " Is it not better
to be freed from cares and agues, love and melancholy, and
the other hot and cold fits of life, than, like a galled traveller who comes weary to his inn, to be bound to begin
his journey afresh ?" Then, closing his Burton and opening his Bacon at the *Essay on Death*, he adds : " There is
no terror, brother Toby, in its (Death's) looks but what it
borrows from groans and convulsions, and " (here parody
forces its way in) " the blowing of noses, and the wiping
away of tears with the bottoms of curtains in a sick man's
bed-room ;" and with one more theft from Burton, after
Seneca : " Consider, brother Toby, when we are, death is
not ; and when death is, we are not," this extraordinary
cento of plagiarisms concludes.

Not that this is Sterne's only raid upon the quaint old
writer of whom he has here made such free use. Several
other instances of word for word appropriation might be
quoted from this and the succeeding volumes of *Tristram
Shandy*. The apostrophe to "blessed health," in c. xxxiii.
of vol. v. is taken direct from the *Anatomy of Melancholy ;*
so is the phrase, " He has a gourd for his head and a pip-
pin for his heart," in c. ix. ; so is the jest about Franciscus
Ribera's computation of the amount of cubic space required

by the souls of the lost; so is Hilarion the hermit's comparison of his body with its unruly passions to a kicking
ass. And there is a passage in the *Sentimental Journey*,
the "Fragment in the Abderitans," which shows, Dr.
Ferriar thinks—though it does not seem to me to show
conclusively—that Sterne was unaware that what he was
taking from Burton had been previously taken by Burton
from Lucian.

There is more excuse, in the opinion of the author of the
Illustrations, for the literary thefts of the preacher than
for those of the novelist; since in sermons, Dr. Ferriar
observes drily, " the principal matter must consist of repetitions." But it can hardly, I think, be admitted that the
kind of "repetitions" to which Sterne had recourse in the
pulpit—or, at any rate, in compositions ostensibly prepared
for the pulpit—are quite justifiable. Professor Jebb has
pointed out, in a recent volume of this series, that the description of the tortures of the Inquisition, which so deeply moved Corporal Trim in the famous Sermon on Conscience, was really the work of Bentley; but Sterne has
pilfered more freely from a divine more famous as a
preacher than the great scholar whose words he appropriated on that occasion. " Then shame and grief go with
her," he exclaims in his singular sermon on " The Levite
and his Concubine;" "and wherever she seeks a shelter
may the hand of Justice shut the door against her!" an
exclamation which is taken, as, no doubt, indeed, was the
whole suggestion of the somewhat strange subject, from
the *Contemplations* of Bishop Hall. And so, again, we
find in Sterne's sermon the following:

"Mercy well becomes the heart of all Thy creatures! but most of
Thy servant, a Levite, who offers up so many daily sacrifices to Thee
for the transgressions of Thy people. But to little purpose, he would

add, have I served at Thy altar, where my business was to sue for mercy, had I not learned to practise it."

And in Hall's *Contemplations* the following:

"Mercy becomes well the heart of any man, but most of a Levite. He that had helped to offer so many sacrifices to God for the multitude of every Israelite's sins saw how proportionable it was that man should not hold one sin unpardonable. He had served at the altar to no purpose, if he (whose trade was to sue for mercy) had not at all learned to practise it."

Sterne's twelfth sermon, on the Forgiveness of Injuries, is merely a diluted commentary on the conclusion of Hall's "Contemplation of Joseph." In the sixteenth sermon, the one on Shimei, we find:

"There is no small degree of malicious craft in fixing upon a season to give a mark of enmity and ill will: a word, a look, which at one time would make no impression, at another time wounds the heart, and, like a shaft flying with the wind, pierces deep, which, with its own natural force, would scarce have reached the object aimed at."

This, it is evident, is but slightly altered, and by no means for the better, from the more terse and vigorous language of the Bishop:

"There is no small cruelty in the picking out of a time for mischief: that word would scarce gall at one season which at another killeth. The same shaft flying with the wind pierces deep, which against it can hardly find strength to stick upright."

But enough of these *pièces de conviction*. Indictments for plagiarism are often too hastily laid; but there can be no doubt, I should imagine, in the mind of any reasonable being upon the evidence here cited, that the offence in this case is clearly proved. Nor, I think, can there be much question as to its moral complexion. For the pilferings

from Bishop Hall, at any rate, no shadow of excuse can,
so far as I can see, be alleged.   Sterne could not possibly
plead any better justification for borrowing Hall's thoughts
and phrases and passing them off upon his hearers or readers as original, than he could plead for claiming the au-
thorship of one of the Bishop's benevolent actions and
representing himself to the world as the doer of the good
deed.   In the actual as in the hypothetical case there is a
dishonest appropriation by one man of the credit—in the
former case the intellectual, in the latter the moral credit
—belonging to another : the offence in the actual case being aggravated by the fact that it involves a fraud upon
the purchaser of the sermon, who pays money for what he
may already have in his library.   The plagiarisms from
Burton stand upon a slightly different though not, I
think, a much more defensible footing.   For in this case it
has been urged that Sterne, being desirous of satirizing ped-
antry, was justified in resorting to the actually existent
writings of an antique pedant of real life ; and that since
Mr. Shandy could not be made to talk more like himself
than Burton talked like *him*, it was artistically lawful to
put Burton's exact words into Mr. Shandy's mouth.   It
makes a difference, it may be said, that Sterne is not here
speaking in his own person, as he is in his *Sermons*, but
in the person of one of his characters.   This casuistry,
however, does not seem to me to be sound.   Even as regards the passages from ancient authors, which, while
quoting them from Burton, he tacitly represents to his
readers as taken from his own stores of knowledge, the
excuse is hardly sufficient ; while as regards the original
reflections of the author of the *Anatomy of Melancholy*
it obviously fails to apply at all.   And in any case there
could be no necessity for the omission to acknowledge the

debt. Even admitting that no more characteristic reflections could have been composed for Mr. Shandy than were
actually to be found in Burton, art is not so exacting a
mistress as to compel the artist to plagiarize against his
will. A scrupulous writer, being also as ingenious as
Sterne, could have found some means of indicating the
source from which he was borrowing without destroying
the dramatic illusion of the scene.

But it seems clear enough that Sterne himself was troubled by no conscientious qualms on this subject. Perhaps
the most extraordinary instance of literary effrontery which
was ever met with is the passage in vol. v. c. 1, which
even that seasoned detective Dr. Ferriar is startled into
pronouncing "singular." Burton had complained that
writers were like apothecaries, who "make new mixtures
every day," by "pouring out of one vessel into another."
"We weave," he said, "the same web still, twist the same
rope again and again." And Sterne *incolumi gravitate*
asks: "Shall we forever make new books as apothecaries
make new mixtures, by pouring only out of one vessel into
another? Are we forever to be twisting and untwisting
the same rope, forever on the same track, forever at the
same pace?" And this he writes with the scissors actually
opened in his hand for the almost bodily abstraction of
the passage beginning, "Man, the most excellent and noble creature of the world!" Surely this denunciation of
plagiarism by a plagiarist on the point of setting to work
could only have been written by a man who looked upon
plagiarism as a good joke.

Apart, however, from the moralities of the matter, it
must in fairness be admitted that in most cases Sterne is no
servile copyist. He appropriates other men's thoughts and
phrases, and with them, of course, the credit for the wit,

K   7   10

the truth, the vigour, or the learning which characterizes
them; but he is seldom found, in *Tristram Shandy*, at any
rate, to have transferred them to his own pages out of a
mere indolent inclination to save himself the trouble of
composition.   He takes them less as substitutes than as
groundwork for his own invention—as so much material
for his own inventive powers to work upon; and those
powers do generally work upon them with conspicuous
skill of elaboration.   The series of cuttings, for instance,
which he makes from Burton, on the occasion of Bobby
Shandy's death, are woven into the main tissue of the dialogue with remarkable ingenuity and naturalness; and the
bright strands of his own unborrowed humour fly flashing
across the fabric at every transit of the shuttle.   Or, to
change the metaphor, we may say that in almost every instance the jewels that so glitter in their stolen setting were
cut and set by Sterne himself.   Let us allow that the most
expert of lapidaries is not justified in stealing his settings;
but let us still not forget that the *jewels* are his, or permit
our disapproval of his laxity of principle to make us unjust to his consummate skill.

CHAPTER X.

STYLE AND GENERAL CHARACTERISTICS.—HUMOUR AND SENTIMENT.

To talk of "the style" of Sterne is almost to play one of those tricks with language of which he himself was so fond. For there is hardly any definition of the word which can make it possible to describe him as having any style at all. It is not only that he manifestly recognized no external canons whereto to conform the expression of his thoughts, but he had, apparently, no inclination to invent and observe—except, indeed, in the most negative of senses—any style of his own. The "style of Sterne," in short, is as though one should say "the form of Proteus." He was determined to be uniformly eccentric, regularly irregular, and that was all. His digressions, his asides, and his fooleries in general would, of course, have in any case necessitated a certain general jerkiness of manner; but this need hardly have extended itself habitually to the structure of individual sentences, and as a matter of fact he can at times write, as he does for the most part in his *Sermons*, in a style which is not the less vigorous for being fairly correct. But as a rule his mode of expressing himself is destitute of any pretensions to precision; and in many instances it is a perfect marvel of literary slipshod. Nor is there any ground for believing that the

slovenliness was invariably intentional. Sterne's truly
hideous French — French at which even Stratford-atte-
Bowe would have stood aghast—is in itself sufficient evidence of a natural insensibility to grammatical accuracy.
Here there can be no suspicion of designed defiance of
rules; and more than one solecism of rather a serious kind
in his use of English words and phrases affords confirm-
atory testimony to the same point. His punctuation is
fearful and wonderful, even for an age in which the *ra-
tionale* of punctuation was more imperfectly understood
than it is at present; and this, though an apparently slight
matter, is not without value as an indication of ways of
thought. But if we can hardly describe Sterne's style as
being in the literary sense a style at all, it has a very distinct *colloquial* character of its own, and as such it is nearly as much deserving of praise as from the literary point
of view it is open to exception. Chaotic as it is in the syn-
tactical sense, it is a perfectly clear vehicle for the conveyance of thought: we are as rarely at a loss for the meaning
of one of Sterne's sentences as we are, for very different
reasons, for the meaning of one of Macaulay's. And his
language is so full of life and colour, his tone so animated
and vivacious, that we forget we are reading and not *listening*, and we are as little disposed to be exacting in respect
to form as though we were listeners in actual fact. Sterne's
manner, in short, may be that of a bad and careless writer,
but it is the manner of a first-rate talker; and this, of
course, enhances rather than detracts from the unwearying
charm of his wit and humour.

To attempt a precise and final distinction between these
two last-named qualities in Sterne or any one else would
be no very hopeful task, perhaps; but those who have a
keen perception of either find no great difficulty in dis-

criminating, as a matter of feeling, between the two. And
what is true of the qualities themselves is true, *mutatis
mutandis*, of the men by whom they have been most conspicuously displayed.   Some wits have been humourists
also ; nearly all humourists have been also wits ; yet the
two fall, on the whole, into tolerably well-marked classes,
and the ordinary uncritical judgment would, probably, en-
able most men to state with sufficient certainty the class to
which each famous name in the world's literature belongs.
Aristophanes, Shakspeare, Cervantes, Molière, Swift, Fielding, Lamb, Richter, Carlyle : widely as these writers differ
from each other in style and genius, the least skilled reader would hardly need to be told that the list which includes
them all is a catalogue of humourists.   And Cicero, Lucian, Pascal, Voltaire, Congreve, Pope, Sheridan, Courier,
Sydney Smith — this, I suppose, would be recognized at
once as an enumeration of wits.   Some of these humourists, like Fielding, like Richter, like Carlyle, are always, or
almost always, humourists alone.   Some of these wits, like
Pascal, like Pope, like Courier, are wits with no, or but
slight, admixture of humour ; and in the classification of
these there is of course no difficulty at all.   But even with
the wits who very often give us humour also, and with the
humourists who as often delight us with their wit, we seldom find ourselves in any doubt as to the real and more
essential affinities of each.   It is not by the wit which he
has infused into his talk, so much as by the humour with
which he has delineated the character, that Shakspeare
has given his Falstaff an abiding place in our memories.
It is not the repartees of Benedick and Beatrice, but the
immortal fatuity of Dogberry, that the name of *Much Ado
About Nothing* recalls.   None of the verbal quips of Touch-
stone tickle us like his exquisite patronage of William and

the fascination which he exercises over the melancholy
Jaques. And it is the same throughout all Shakspeare.
It is of the humours of Bottom, and Launce, and Shallow,
and Sly, and Aguecheek; it is of the laughter that treads
upon the heels of horror and pity and awe, as we listen to
the Porter in *Macbeth*, to the Grave-digger in *Hamlet*, to
the Fool in *Lear*—it is of these that we think when we
think of Shakspeare in any other but his purely poetic mood.
Whenever, that is to say, we think of him as anything but
a poet, we think of him, not as a wit, but as a humourist.
So, too, it is not the dagger-thrusts of the *Drapier's Letters*,
but the broad ridicule of the *Voyage to Laputa*, the savage
irony of the *Voyage to the Houyhnhnms*, that we associate
with the name of Swift. And, conversely, it is the cold,
epigrammatic glitter of Congreve's dialogue, the fizz and
crackle of the fireworks which Sheridan serves out with un-
discriminating hand to the most insignificant of his characters—it is this which stamps the work of these dramatists
with characteristics far more marked than any which belong to them in right of humorous portraiture of human
foibles or ingenious invention of comic incident.

The place of Sterne is unmistakably among writers of
the former class. It is by his humour—his humour of
character, his dramatic as distinct from his critical de-
scriptive *personal* humour—though, of course, he possesses
this also, as all humourists must—that he lives and will live.
In *Tristram Shandy*, as in the *Sermons*, there is a sufficiency of wit, and considerably more than a sufficiency of
humorous reflection, innuendo, and persiflage; but it is the
actors in his almost plotless drama who have established
their creator in his niche in the Temple of Fame. We
cannot, indeed, be sure that what has given him his hold
upon posterity is what gave him his popularity with his

contemporaries. On the contrary, it is, perhaps, more
probable that he owed his first success with the public of
his day to those eccentricities which are for us a little too
consciously eccentric—those artifices which fail a little too
conspicuously in the *ars celandi artem*. But however these
tricks may have pleased in days when such tricks were new,
they much more often weary than divert us now; and I
suspect that many a man whose delight in the Corporal
and his master, in Bridget and her mistress, is as fresh as
ever, declines to accompany their creator in those perpetual digressions into nonsense or semi-nonsense the fashion
of which Sterne borrowed from Rabelais, without Rabelais's excuse for adopting it. To us of this day the real
charm and distinction of the book is due to the marvellous
combination of vigour and subtlety in its portrayal of
character, and in the purity and delicacy of its humour.
Those last two apparently paradoxical substantives are
chosen advisedly, and employed as the most convenient
way of introducing that disagreeable question which no
commentator on Sterne can possibly shirk, but which every admirer of Sterne must approach with reluctance.
There is, of course, a sense in which Sterne's humour—
if, indeed, we may bestow that name on the form of jocu-
larity to which I refer—is the very reverse of pure and
delicate : a sense in which it is impure and indelicate in
the highest degree. On this it is necessary, however brief-
ly, to touch; and to the weighty and many-counted in-
dictment which may be framed against Sterne on this
head there is, of course, but one possible plea—the plea
of guilty. Nay, the plea must go further than a mere
admission of the offence; it must include an admission
of the worst motive, the worst spirit as animating the offender. It is not necessary to my purpose, nor doubtless

congenial to the taste of the reader, that I should enter
upon any critical analysis of this quality in the author's
work, or compare him in this respect with the two other great humourists who have been the worst offenders
in the same way. In one of those highly interesting criticisms of English literature which, even when they most
conspicuously miss the mark, are so instructive to Englishmen, M. Taine has instituted an elaborate comparison—very
much, I need hardly say, to the advantage of the latter—
between the indecency of Swift and that of Rabelais—
that "good giant," as his countryman calls him, "who
rolls himself joyously about on his dunghill, thinking no
evil." And no doubt the world of literary moralists will
always be divided upon the question—one mainly of na-
tional temperament—whether mere animal spirits or serious satiric purpose is the best justification for offences
against cleanliness. It is, of course, only the former theory, if either, which could possibly avail Sterne, and it would
need an unpleasantly minute analysis of this characteristic
in his writings to ascertain how far M. Taine's eloquent
defence of Rabelais could be made applicable to his case.
But the inquiry, one is glad to think, is as unnecessary as
it would be disagreeable; for, unfortunately for Sterne, he
must be condemned on a *quantitative* comparison of indecency, whatever may be his fate when compared with
these other two great writers as regards the quality of
their respective transgressions. There can be no denying,
I mean, that Sterne is of all writers the most permeated
and penetrated with impurity of thought and suggestion;
that in no other writer is its latent presence more constantly felt, even if there be any in whom it is more often
openly obtruded. The unclean spirit pursues him every-
where, disfiguring his scenes of humour, demoralizing his

passages of serious reflection, debasing even his sentimental interludes. His coarseness is very often as great
a blot on his art as on his morality—a thing which can
very rarely be said of either Swift or Rabelais; and it is
sometimes so distinctly fatal a blemish from the purely
literary point of view, that one is amazed at the critical
faculty which could have tolerated its presence.

But when all this has been said of Sterne's humour it
still remains true that, in another sense of the words "purity." and "delicacy," he possesses humour more pure and
delicate than, perhaps, any other writer in the world can
show. For if that humour is the purest and most delicate which is the freest from any admixture of farce, and
produces its effects with the lightest touch, and the least
obligations to ridiculous incident, or what may be called
the "physical grotesque," in any shape—then one can
point to passages from Sterne's pen which, for fulfilment
of these conditions, it would be difficult to match elsewhere. Strange as it may seem to say this of the literary
Gilray who drew the portrait of Dr. Slop, and of the literary Grimaldi who tormented Phutatorius with the hot
chestnut, it is nevertheless the fact that scene after scene
may be cited from *Tristram Shandy*, and those the most
delightful in the book, which are not only free from even
the momentary intrusion of either the clown or the carica-
turist, but even from the presence of "comic properties"
(as actors would call them) of any kind: scenes of which
the external setting is of the simplest possible character,
while the humour is of that deepest and most penetrative
kind which springs from the eternal incongruities of human nature, the ever-recurring cross-purposes of human
lives.

Carlyle classes Sterne with Cervantes among the great
7*

humourists of the world; and from one, and that the most important, point of view the praise is not extravagant. By no other writer besides Sterne, perhaps, since the days of the Spanish humourist, have the vast incongruities of human character been set forth with so masterly a hand. It is in virtue of the new insight which his humour opens to us of the immensity and variety of man's life that Cervantes makes us feel that he is *great:* not delightful merely—not even eternally delightful only, and secure of immortality through the perennial human need of joy—but *great*, but immortal, in right of that which makes Shakspeare and the Greek dramatists immortal, namely, the power, not alone over the pleasure-loving part of man's nature, but over that equally universal but more enduring element in it, his emotions of wonder and of awe. It is to this greater power—this control over a greater instinct than the human love of joy, that Cervantes owes his greatness; and it will be found, though it may seem at first a hard saying, that Sterne shares this power with Cervantes. To pass from Quixote and Sancho to Walter and Toby Shandy involves, of course, a startling change of dramatic key—a notable lowering of dramatic tone. It is almost like passing from poetry to prose: it is certainly passing from the poetic in spirit and surroundings to the profoundly prosaic in fundamental conception and in every individual detail. But those who do not allow accidental and external dissimilarities to obscure for them the inward and essential resemblances of things, must often, I think, have experienced from one of the Shandy dialogues the same *sort* of impression that they derive from some of the most nobly humorous colloquies between the knight and his squire, and must have been conscious through all outward differences of key and tone

of a common element in each. It is, of course, a resemblance of *relations* and not of personalities; for though
there is something of the Knight of La Mancha in Mr.
Shandy, there is nothing of Sancho about his brother.
But the serio-comic game of cross-purposes is the same
between both couples ; and what one may call the irony
of human intercourse is equally profound, and pointed
with equal subtlety, in each. In the Spanish romance, of
course, it is not likely to be missed. It is enough in itself
that the deranged brain which takes windmills for giants,
and carriers for knights, and Rosinante for a Bucephalus,
has fixed upon Sancho Panza—the crowning proof of its
mania—as the fitting squire of a knight-errant. To him
—to this compound of somnolence, shrewdness, and good
nature—to this creature with no more tincture of romantic
idealism than a wine-skin, the knight addresses, without
misgiving, his lofty dissertations on the glories and the
duties of chivalry—the squire responding after his fashion. And thus these two hold converse, contentedly in-
comprehensible to each other, and with no suspicion that
they are as incapable of interchanging ideas as the inhabitants of two different planets. With what heart-
stirring mirth, and yet with what strangely deeper feeling of the infinite variety of human nature, do we follow
their converse throughout ! Yet Quixote and Sancho are
not more life-like and human, nor nearer together at one
point and farther apart at another, than are Walter
Shandy and his brother. The squat little Spanish peasant
is not more gloriously incapable of following the chivalric
vagaries of his master than the simple soldier is of grasping the philosophic crotchets of his brother. Both couples
are in sympathetic contact absolute and complete at one
point ; at another they are " poles asunder " both of them.

And in both contrasts there is that sense of futility and failure, of alienation and misunderstanding—that element of underlying pathos, in short, which so strangely gives its keenest salt to humour. In both alike there is the same suggestion of the Infinite of disparity bounding the finite of resemblance—of the Incommensurable in man and nature, beside which all minor uniformities sink into insignificance.

The pathetic element which underlies and deepens the humour is, of course, produced in the two cases in two exactly opposite ways. In both cases it is a picture of human simplicity—of a noble and artless nature out of harmony with its surroundings—which moves us ; but whereas in the Spanish romance the simplicity is that of the *incompris,* in the English novel it is that of the man with whom the *incompris* consorts. If there is pathos as well as humour, and deepening the humour, in the figure of the distraught knight-errant talking so hopelessly over the head of his attached squire's morality, so too there is pathos, giving depth to the humour of the eccentric philosopher, shooting so hopelessly wide of the intellectual appreciation of the most affectionate of brothers. One's sympathy, perhaps, is even more strongly appealed to in the latter than in the former case, because the effort of the good Captain to understand is far greater than that of the Don to make himself understood, and the concern of the former at his failure is proportionately more marked than that of the latter at *his.* And the general *rapport* between one of the two ill-assorted pairs is much closer than that of the other. It is, indeed, the tantalizing approach to a mutual understanding which gives so much more subtle a zest to the humour of the relations between the two brothers Shandy than to that which arises out of the re-

lations between the philosopher and his wife. The broad
comedy of the dialogues between Mr. and Mrs. Shandy is
irresistible in its way: but it *is* broad comedy. The
philosopher knows that his wife does not comprehend
him: she knows that she never will; and neither of them
much cares. The husband snubs her openly for her mental
defects, and she with perfect placidity accepts his rebukes.
"Master," as he once complains, "of one of the finest
chains of reasoning in the world, he is unable for the soul
of him to get a single link of it into the head of his wife;"
but we never hear him lamenting in this serio-comic fashion over his brother's inability to follow his processes of
reasoning. That is too serious a matter with both of
them; their mutual desire to share each other's ideas and
tastes is too strong; and each time that the philosopher
shows his impatience with the soldier's fortification-hobby,
or the soldier breaks his honest shins over one of the philosopher's crotchets, the regret and remorse on either side
is equally acute and sincere. It must be admitted, however, that Captain Shandy is the one who the more frequently subjects himself to pangs of this sort, and who is
the more innocent sufferer of the two.

From the broad and deep humour of this central conception of contrast flow as from a head-water innumerable
rills of comedy through many and many a page of dialogue; but not, of course, from this source alone. Uncle
Toby is ever delightful, even when his brother is not near
him as his foil; the faithful Corporal brings out another
side of his character, upon which we linger with equal
pleasure of contemplation; the allurements of the Widow
Wadman reveal him to us in yet another—but always in a
captivating aspect. There is, too, one need hardly say, an
abundance of humour, of a high, though not the highest,

order in the minor characters of the story—in Mrs. Shandy, in the fascinating widow, and even, under the coarse
lines of the physical caricature, in the keen little Catholic,
Slop himself.   But it is in Toby Shandy alone that humour reaches that supreme level which it is only capable
of attaining when the collision of contrasted qualities in a
human character produces a corresponding conflict of the
emotions of mirth and tenderness in the minds of those
who contemplate it.

This, however, belongs more rightfully to the consideration of the creative and dramatic element in Sterne's genius; and an earlier place in the analysis is claimed by
that power over the emotion of pity upon which Sterne,
beyond question, prided himself more highly than upon
any other of his gifts.   He preferred, we can plainly see,
to think of himself, not as the great humourist, but as the
great sentimentalist; and though the word "sentiment"
had something even in *his* day of the depreciatory meaning which distinguishes it nowadays from "pathos," there
can be little doubt that the thing appeared to Sterne to be,
on the whole, and both in life and literature, rather admirable than the reverse.

What, then, were his notions of true "sentiment" in
literature?   We have seen elsewhere that he repeats—it
would appear unconsciously—and commends the canon
which Horace propounds to the tragic poet in the words:

"Si vis me flere, dolendum
Primum ipsi tibi: tunc tua me infortunia lædent."

And that canon is sound enough, no doubt, in the sense
in which it was meant, and in its relation to the person to
whom it was addressed.   A tragic drama, peopled with
heroes who set forth their woes in frigid and unimpas-

sioned verse, will unquestionably leave its audience as cold
as itself. Nor is this true of drama alone. All *poetry*,
indeed, whether dramatic or other, presupposes a sympathetic unity of emotion between the poet and those whom
he addresses; and to this extent it is obviously true that
he must feel before they can. Horace, who was (what
every literary critic is not) a man of the world and an
observer of human nature, did not, of course, mean that
this capacity for feeling was all, or even the chief part, of
the poetic faculty. He must have seen many an "intense"
young Roman make that pathetic error of the young in all
countries and of all periods—the error of mistaking the
capacity of emotion for the gift of expression. He did,
however, undoubtedly mean that a poet's power of affect-
ing others presupposes passion in himself; and, as regards
the poet, he was right. But his criticism takes no account
whatever of one form of appeal to the emotions which has
been brought by later art to a high pitch of perfection,
but with which the personal feeling of the artist has not
much more to do than the "passions" of an auctioneer's
clerk have to do with the compilation of his inventory. A
poet himself, Horace wrote for poets; to him the pathetic
implied the ideal, the imaginative, the rhetorical; he lived
before the age of Realism and the Realists, and would
scarcely have comprehended either the men or the method
if he could have come across them. Had he done so, however, he would have been astonished to find his canon re-
versed, and to have perceived that the primary condition
of the realist's success, and the distinctive note of those
writers who have pressed genius into the service of realism, is that they do *not* share—that they are unalterably
and ostentatiously free from—the emotions to which they
appeal in their readers. A fortunate accident has enabled

us to compare the treatment which the world's greatest
tragic poet and its greatest master of realistic tragedy have
respectively applied to virtually the same subject; and the
two methods are never likely to be again so impressively
contrasted as in *King Lear* and *Le Père Goriot.* But, in
truth, it must be impossible for any one who feels Balzac's
power not to feel also how it is heightened by Balzac's
absolute calm—a calm entirely different from that stern
composure which was merely a point of style and not an
attitude of the heart with the old Greek tragedians—a
calm which, unlike theirs, insulates, so to speak, and is intended to insulate, the writer, to the end that his individu-
ality, of which only the electric current of sympathy ever
makes a reader conscious, may disappear, and the characters of the drama stand forth the more life-like from the
complete concealment of the hand that moves them.

Of this kind of art Horace, as has been said, knew nothing, and his canon only applies to it by the rule of contra-
ries. Undoubtedly, and in spite of the marvels which one
great genius has wrought with it, it is a form lower than
the poetic — essentially a prosaic, and in many or most
hands an unimaginative, form of art; but for this very reason, that it demands nothing of its average practitioner
but a keen eye for facts, great and small, and a knack of
graphically recording them, it has become a far more commonly and successfully cultivated form of art than any
other. As to the question who *are* its practitioners, it
would, of course, be the merest dogmatism to commit
one's self to any attempt at rigid classification in such a
matter. There are few if any writers who can be described without qualification either as realists or as idealists.
Nearly all of them, probably, are realists at one moment
and in one mood, and idealists at other moments and in

other moods. All that need be insisted on is that the
methods of the two forms of art are essentially distinct,
and that artistic failure must result from any attempt to
combine them ; for, whereas the primary condition of success in the one case is that the reader should feel the sympathetic presence of the writer, the primary condition of
success in the other is that the writer should efface himself from the reader's consciousness altogether. And it is,
I think, the defiance of these conditions which explains
why so much of Sterne's deliberately pathetic writing is,
from the artistic point of view, a failure. It is this which
makes one feel so much of it to be strained and unnatural,
and which brings it to pass that some of his most ambitious efforts leave the reader indifferent, or even now and
then contemptuous. In those passages of pathos in which
the effect is distinctly sought by realistic means Sterne is
perpetually ignoring the "self-denying ordinance" of his
adopted method—perpetually obtruding his own individu-
ality, and begging us, as it were, to turn from the picture
to the artist, to cease gazing for a moment at his touching
creation, and to admire the fine feeling, the exquisitely
sympathetic nature of the man who created it. No doubt,
as we must in fairness remember, it was part of his "humour"—in Ancient Pistol's sense of the word—to do this ;
it is true, no doubt (and a truth which Sterne's most famous critic was too prone to ignore), that his sentiment is
not always *meant* for serious ;[1] nay, the very word "senti-

[1] Surely it was not so meant, for instance, in the passage about
the *désobligeante*, which had been "standing so many months unpitied
in the corner of Monsieur Dessein's coach-yard. Much, indeed, was
not to be said for it, but something might; and, when a few words
will rescue Misery out of her distress, I hate the man who can be a
churl of them." "Does anybody," asks Thackeray in strangely mat-

mental" itself, though in Sterne's day, of course, it had
acquired but a part of its present disparaging significance,
is a sufficient proof of that. But there are, nevertheless,
plenty of passages, both in *Tristram Shandy* and the *Sentimental Journey*, where the intention is wholly and un-
mixedly pathetic—where the smile is not for a moment
meant to compete with the tear—which are, nevertheless,
it must be owned, complete failures, and failures traceable
with much certainty, or so it seems to me, to the artistic
error above-mentioned.

In one famous case, indeed, the failure can hardly be described as other than ludicrous. The figure of the distraught Maria of Moulines is tenderly drawn; the accessories of the picture—her goat, her dog, her pipe, her song
to the Virgin—though a little theatrical, perhaps, are skilfully touched in; and so long as the Sentimental Traveller
keeps our attention fixed upon her and them the scene
prospers well enough. But, after having bidden us duly
note how "the tears trickled down her cheeks," the Traveller continues: "I sat down close by her, and Maria let
me wipe them away as they fell with my handkerchief.
I then steeped it in my own—and then in hers—and then
in mine—and then I wiped hers again; and as I did it I
felt such undescribable emotions within me as, I am sure,
could not be accounted for from any combinations of matter and motion." The reader of this may well ask himself in wonderment whether he is really expected to make

ter-of-fact fashion, "believe that this is a real sentiment? that this
luxury of generosity, this gallant rescue of Misery—out of an old
cab—is genuine feeling?" Nobody, we should say. But, on the
other hand, does anybody—or did anybody before Thackeray—sug-
gest that it was meant to pass for genuine feeling? Is it not an obvious piece of mock pathetic?

a third in the lachrymose group. We look at the passage
again, and more carefully, to see if, after all, we may not
be intended to laugh, and not to cry at it; but on finding,
as clearly appears, that we actually *are* intended to cry at
it the temptation to laugh becomes almost irresistible.
We proceed, however, to the account of Maria's wanderings to Rome and back, and we come to the pretty passage
which follows:

> "How she had borne it, and how she had got supported, she could
> not tell; but God tempers the wind, said Maria, to the shorn lamb.
> Shorn indeed! and to the quick, said I; and wast thou in my own
> land, where I have a cottage, I would take thee to it, and shelter thee;
> thou shouldst eat of my own bread and drink of my own cup; I
> would be kind to thy Sylvio; in all thy weaknesses and wanderings
> I would seek after thee, and bring thee back. When the sun went
> down I would say my prayers; and when I had done thou shouldst
> play thy evening-song upon thy pipe; nor would the incense of my
> sacrifice be worse accepted for entering heaven along with that of a
> broken heart."

But then follows more whimpering:

> "Nature melted within me [continues Sterne] as I said this; and
> Maria observing, as I took out my handkerchief, that it was steeped
> too much already to be of use, would needs go wash it in the stream.
> And where will you dry it, Maria? said I. I'll dry it in my bosom,
> said she; 'twill do me good. And is your heart still so warm, Maria?
> said I. I touched upon the string on which hung all her sorrows.
> She looked with wistful disorder for some time in my face; and then,
> without saying anything, took her pipe and played her service to the
> Virgin."

Which are we meant to look at—the sorrows of Maria?
or the sensibilities of the Sentimental Traveller? or the
condition of the pocket-handkerchief? I think it doubtful whether any writer of the first rank has ever perpe-
trated so disastrous a literary failure as this scene; but the

main cause of that failure appears to me not doubtful at all. The artist has no business within the frame of the picture, and his intrusion into it has spoilt it. The method adopted from the commencement is ostentatiously objective: we are taken straight into Maria's presence, and bidden to look at and to pity the unhappy maiden as *described* by the Traveller who met her. No attempt is made to place us at the outset in sympathy with *him;* he, until he thrusts himself before us, with his streaming eyes, and his drenched pocket-handkerchief, is a mere reporter of the scene before him, and he and his tears are as much out of place as if he were the compositor who set up the type. It is not merely that we don't want to know how the scene affected him, and that we resent as an impertinence the elaborate account of his tender emotions; we don't wish to be reminded of his presence at all. For, as we can know nothing (effectively) of Maria's sorrows except as given in her appearance—the historical recital of them and their cause being too curt and bald to be able to move us—the best chance for moving our compassion for her is to make the illusion of her presence as dramatically real as possible; a chance which is, therefore, completely destroyed when the author of the illusion insists on thrusting himself between ourselves and the scene.

But, in truth, this whole episode of Maria of Moulines was, like more than one of Sterne's efforts after the pathetic, condemned to failure from the very conditions of its birth. These abortive efforts are no natural growth of his artistic genius; they proceed rather from certain morbidly stimulated impulses of his moral nature which he forced his artistic genius to subserve. He had true pathetic power, simple yet subtle, at his command; but it visited him unsought, and by inspiration from without.

It came when he was in the dramatic and not in the in-
trospective mood; when he was thinking honestly of his
characters, and not of himself. But he was, unfortunately,
too prone — and a long course of moral self-indulgence
had confirmed him in it—to the habit of caressing his
own sensibilities; and the result of this was always to set
him upon one of those attempts to be pathetic of *malice
prepense* of which Maria of Moulines is one example, and
the too celebrated dead donkey of Nampont another. "It
is agreeably and skilfully done, that dead jackass," writes
Thackeray; "like M. de Soubise's cook on the campaign,
Sterne dresses it, and serves it up quite tender, and with
a very piquante sauce. But tears, and fine feelings, and
a white pocket-handkerchief, and a funeral sermon, and
horses and feathers, and a procession of mutes, and a
hearse with a dead donkey inside! Psha! Mounte-
bank! I'll not give thee one penny-piece for that trick,
donkey and all." That is vigorous ridicule, and not wholly undeserved; but, on the other hand, not entirely deserved. There is less of artistic trick, it seems to me, and
more of natural foible, about Sterne's literary sentiment
than Thackeray was ever willing to believe; and I can find
nothing worse, though nothing better, in the dead ass of
Nampont than in Maria of Moulines. I do not think there
is any conscious simulation of feeling in this Nampont
scene; it is that the feeling itself is overstrained—that
Sterne, hugging, as usual, his own sensibilities, mistook
their value in expression for the purposes of art. The
Sentimental Traveller does not obtrude himself to the
same extent as in the scene at Moulines; but a little consideration of the scene will show how much Sterne relied on the mere presentment of the fact that here was
an unfortunate peasant who had lost his dumb companion,

and here a tender-hearted gentleman looking on and pity-
ing him. As for any attempts to bring out, by objective
dramatic touches, either the grievousness of the bereave-
ment or the grief of the mourner, such attempts as are
made to do this are either commonplace or "one step in
advance" of the sublime. Take this, for instance: "The
mourner was sitting upon a stone bench at the door, with
his ass's pannel and its bridle on one side, which he took
up from time to time, then laid them down, looked at
them, and shook his head. He then took the crust of
bread out of his wallet again, as if to eat it; held it some
time in his hand, then laid it upon the bit of his ass's
bridle—looked wistfully at the little arrangement he had
made—and then gave a sigh. The simplicity of his grief
drew numbers about him," &c. Simplicity, indeed, of a
marvellous sort which could show itself by so extraordinary a piece of acting as this! Is there any critic who candid-
ly thinks it natural—I do not mean in the sense of mere
every-day probability, but of conformity to the laws of human character? Is it true that in any country, among any
people, however emotional, grief—real, unaffected, un-self-
conscious grief—ever did or ever could display itself by
such a trick as that of laying a piece of bread on the bit
of a dead ass's bridle? Do we not feel that if we had
been on the point of offering comfort or alms to the
mourner, and saw him go through this extraordinary piece
of pantomime, we should have buttoned up our hearts
and pockets forthwith? Sentiment, again, sails very near
the wind of the ludicrous in the reply to the Traveller's
remark that the mourner had been a merciful master to
the dead ass. "Alas!" the latter says, "I thought so when
he was alive, but now that he is dead I think otherwise.
I fear the weight of *myself and my afflictions* have been

too much for him." And the scene ends flatly enough
with the scrap of morality: "'Shame on the world!' said
I to myself. 'Did we love each other as this poor soul
loved his ass, 'twould be something.'"

The whole incident, in short, is one of those examples
of the deliberate-pathetic with which Sterne's highly natural
art had least, and his highly artificial nature most, to do.
He is never so unsuccessful as when, after formally announc-
ing, as it were, that he means to be touching, he proceeds
to select his subject, to marshal his characters, to group his
accessories, and with painful and painfully apparent elaboration to work up his scene to the weeping point. There is
no obviousness of suggestion, no spontaneity of treatment
about this "Dead Ass" episode; indeed, there is some
reason to believe that it was one of those most hopeless of
efforts—the attempt at the mechanical repetition of a former triumph. It is by no means improbable, at any rate, that
the dead ass of Nampont owes its presence in the *Sentimental Journey* to the reception met with by the live ass of
Lyons in the seventh volume of *Tristram Shandy*. And yet
what an astonishing difference between the two sketches!

"'Twas a poor ass, who had just turned in, with a couple of large
panniers upon his back, to collect eleemosynary turnip-tops and cab-
bage-leaves, and stood dubious with his two fore-feet on the inside of
the threshold, and with his two hinder feet towards the street, as not
knowing very well whether he would go in or no. Now, 'tis an animal (be in what hurry I may) I cannot bear to strike. There is a
patient endurance of sufferings wrote so unaffectedly in his looks and
carriage, which pleads so mightily for him that it always disarms me,
and to that degree that I do not like to speak unkindly to him; on
the contrary, meet him where I will, in town or country, in cart or
under panniers, whether in liberty or bondage, I have ever something
civil to say to him on my part; and, as one word begets another (if
he has as little to do as I), I generally fall into conversation with him;

and surely never is my imagination so busy as in framing his re-
sponses from the etchings of his countenance—and where those
carry me not deep enough, in flying from my own heart into his,
and feeling what is natural for an ass to think, as well as a man,
upon the occasion. . . . Come, Honesty! said I, seeing it was im-
practicable to pass betwixt him and the gate, art thou for coming in
or going out ? The ass twisted his head round, to look up the street.
Well, replied I, we'll wait a minute for thy driver. He turned his
head thoughtfully about, and looked wistfully the opposite way. I
understand thee perfectly, answered I : if thou takest a wrong step
in this affair he will cudgel thee to death. Well, a minute is but a
minute, and if it saves a fellow-creature a drubbing, it shall not be
set down as ill spent. He was eating the stem of an artichoke as
this discourse went on, and, in the little peevish contentions of nature betwixt hunger and unsavouriness, had dropped it out of his
mouth half a dozen times, and picked it up again. God help thee,
Jack ! said I, thou hast a bitter breakfast on't, and many a bitter
blow, I fear, for its wages—'tis all, all bitterness to thee, whatever
life is to others. And now thy mouth, if one knew the truth of it, is
as bitter, I dare say, as soot (for he had cast aside the stem), and
thou hast not a friend, perhaps, in all this world that will give thee a
macaroon. In saying this I pulled out a paper of 'em, which I had
just purchased, and gave him one; and, at this moment that I am
telling it, my heart smites me that there was more of pleasantry in
the conceit of seeing how an ass would eat a macaroon, than of benevolence in giving him one, which presided in the act. When the
ass had eaten his macaroon I pressed him to come in. The poor
beast was heavy loaded, his legs seemed to tremble under him, he
hung rather backwards, and as I pulled at his halter it broke short
in my hand. He looked up pensive in my face. 'Don't thrash me
with it ; but if you will, you may.' 'If I do,' said I, ' I'll be d——d.' "

Well might Thackeray say of this passage that, " the
critic who refuses to see in it wit, humour, pathos, a kind
nature speaking, and a real sentiment, must be hard indeed to move and to please." It is, in truth, excellent ;
and its excellence is due to its possessing nearly every one
of those qualities, positive and negative, which the two

other scenes above quoted are without. The author does
not here obtrude himself, does not importune us to admire
his exquisitely compassionate nature ; on the contrary, he
at once amuses us and enlists our sympathies by that
subtly humorous piece of self-analysis, in which he shows
how large an admixture of curiosity was contained in his
benevolence. The incident, too, is well chosen. No forced
concurrence of circumstances brings it about : it is such as
any man might have met with anywhere in his travels, and
it is handled in a simple and manly fashion. The reader
is *with* the writer throughout ; and their common mood of
half-humorous pity is sustained, unforced, but unbroken,
from first to last.

One can hardly say as much for another of the much-
quoted pieces from the *Sentimental Journey*—the description of the caged starling. The passage is ingeniously
worked into its context ; and if we were to consider it as
only intended to serve the purpose of a sudden and dramatic discomfiture of the Traveller's somewhat inconsider-
ate moralizings on captivity, it would be well enough.
But, regarded as a substantive appeal to one's emotions,
it is open to the criticisms which apply to most other of
Sterne's too deliberate attempts at the pathetic. The details of the picture are too much insisted on, and there is
too much of self-consciousness in the artist. Even at the
very close of the story of Le Fevre's death—finely told
though, as a whole, it is—there is a jarring note. Even
while the dying man is breathing his last our sleeve is
twitched as we stand at his bedside, and our attention
forcibly diverted from the departing soldier to the literary
ingenuities of the man who is describing his end :

"There was a frankness in my Uncle Toby, not the effect of familiarity, but the cause of it, which let you at once into his soul, and
8

showed you the goodness of his nature. To this there was something in his looks, and voice, and manner, superadded, which eternally beck-oned to the unfortunate to come and take shelter under him ; so that before my Uncle Toby had half finished the kind offers he was mak-ing to the father had the son insensibly pressed up close to his knees, and had taken hold of the breast of his coat, and was pulling it to-wards him. The blood and spirits of Le Fevre, which were waxing cold and slow within him, and were retreating to their last citadel, the heart, rallied back ; the film forsook his eyes for a moment ; he looked up wishfully in my Uncle Toby's face, then cast a look upon his boy—and that ligament, fine as it was, was never broken."

How excellent all that is ! and how perfectly would the scene have ended had it closed with the tender and poetic image which thus describes the dying soldier's commenda-tion of his orphan boy to the care of his brother-in-arms ! But what of this, which closes the scene, in fact ?

"Nature instantly ebbed again ; the film returned to its place ; the pulse fluttered — stopped — went on — throbbed — stopped again — moved, stopped. Shall I go on ? No."

Let those admire this who can. To me I confess it seems to spoil a touching and simple death-bed scene by a piece of theatrical trickery.

The sum, in fact, of the whole matter appears to be, that the sentiment on which Sterne so prided himself—-the acute sensibilities which he regarded with such extraordi-nary complacency, were, as has been before observed, the weakness, and not the strength, of his pathetic style. When Sterne the artist is uppermost, when he is survey-ing his characters with that penetrating eye of his, and above all when he is allowing his subtle and tender hu-mour to play upon them unrestrained, he can touch the springs of compassionate emotion in us with a potent and unerring hand. But when Sterne the man is uppermost—

when he is looking inward and not outward, contemplating his own feelings instead of those of his personages, his cunning fails him altogether.   He is at his best in pathos when he is most the humourist; or rather, we may almost say, his pathos is never good unless when it is closely interwoven with his humour.   In this, of course, there is nothing at all surprising.   The only marvel is, that a man who was such a master of the humorous, in its highest and deepest sense, should seem to have so little understood how near together lie the sources of tears and laughter on the very way-side of man's mysterious life.

CHAPTER XI.

CREATIVE AND DRAMATIC POWER.—PLACE IN ENGLISH LITERATURE.

SUBTLE as is Sterne's humour, and true as, in its proper moods, is his pathos, it is not to these but to the parent gift from which they sprang, and perhaps to only one special display of that gift, that he owes his immortality. We are accustomed to bestow so lightly this last hyperbolic honour—hyperbolic always, even when we are speaking of a Homer or a Shakspeare, if only we project the vision far enough forward through time—that the comparative ease with which it is to be earned has itself come to be exaggerated. There are so many " deathless ones " about —if I may put the matter familiarly—in conversation and in literature, that we get into the way of thinking that they are really a considerable body in actual fact, and that the works which have triumphed over death are far more numerous still. The real truth, however, is, that not only are "those who reach posterity a very select company indeed," but most of them have come much nearer missing their destiny than is popularly supposed. Of the dozen or score of writers in one century whom their own contemporaries fondly decree immortal, one-half, perhaps, may be remembered in the next; while of the creations which were honoured with the diploma of immortality a very

much smaller proportion as a rule survive. Only some
fifty per cent. of the prematurely laurel-crowned reach the
goal; and often even upon *their* brows there flutter but a
few stray leaves of the bay. A single poem, a solitary
drama—nay, perhaps one isolated figure, poetic or dramatic—avails, and but barely avails, to keep the immortal
from putting on mortality. Hence we need think it no
disparagement to Sterne to say that he lives not so much
in virtue of his creative power as of one great individual
creation. His imaginative insight into character in general was, no doubt, considerable; his draughtsmanship,
whether as exhibited in the rough sketch or in the finished
portrait, is unquestionably most vigorous; but an artist
may put a hundred striking figures upon his canvas for
one that will linger in the memory of those who have gazed
upon it; and it is, after all, I think, the one figure of Captain Tobias Shandy which has graven itself indelibly on
the memory of mankind. To have made this single addition to the imperishable types of human character em-
bodied in the world's literature may seem, as has been said,
but a light matter to those who talk with light exaggera-
tion of the achievements of the literary artist; but if we
exclude that one creative prodigy among men, who has
peopled a whole gallery with imaginary beings more real
than those of flesh and blood, we shall find that very few
archetypal creations have sprung from any single hand.
Now, My Uncle Toby is as much the archetype of guile-
less good nature, of affectionate simplicity, as Hamlet is of
irresolution, or Iago of cunning, or Shylock of race-hatred;
and he contrives to preserve all the characteristics of an
ideal type amid surroundings of intensely prosaic realism,
with which he himself, moreover, considered as an individual character in a specific story, is in complete accord. If

any one be disposed to underrate the creative and dramatic
power to which this testifies, let him consider how it has
commonly fared with those writers of prose fiction who
have attempted to personify a virtue in a man. Take the
work of another famous English humourist and sentimentalist, and compare Uncle Toby's manly and dignified gen-
tleness of heart with the unreal "gush" of the Brothers
Cheeryble, or the fatuous benevolence of Mr. Pickwick.
We do not believe in the former, and we cannot but de-
spise the latter. But Captain Shandy is reality itself,
within and without; and though we smile at his naïveté,
and may even laugh outright at his boyish enthusiasm for
his military hobby, we never cease to respect him for a
moment. There is no shirking or softening of the comic
aspects of his character; there could not be, of course, for
Sterne needed him more, and used him more, for his purposes as a humourist than for his purposes as a sentimentalist. Nay, it is on the rare occasions when he deliberately sentimentalizes with Captain Shandy that the Captain is the least delightful; it is then that the hand loses
its cunning, and the stroke strays; it is then, and only
then, that the benevolence of the good soldier seems to
verge, though ever so little, upon affectation. It is a pity,
for instance, that Sterne should, in illustration of Captain
Shandy's kindness of heart, have plagiarized (as he is said
to have done) the incident of the tormenting fly, caught
and put out of the window with the words "Get thee
gone, poor devil! Why should I harm thee? The world
is surely large enough for thee and me." There is something too much of self-conscious virtue in the apostrophe.
This, we feel, is not the real Uncle Toby of Sterne's objective mood; it is the Uncle Toby of the subjectifying sentimentalist, surveying his character through the false me-

dium of his own hypertrophied sensibilities. These lapses, however, are, fortunately, rare. As a rule we see the worthy Captain only as he appeared to his creator's keen dramatic eye, and as he is set before us in a thousand exquisite touches of dialogue—the man of simple mind and soul, profoundly unimaginative and unphilosophical, but lacking not in a certain shrewd common-sense; exquisitely *naïf*, and delightfully *mal-à-propos* in his observations, but always pardonably, never foolishly, so; inexhaustibly amiable, but with no weak amiability; homely in his ways, but a perfect gentleman withal; in a word, the most winning and lovable personality that is to be met with, surely, in the whole range of fiction.

It is, in fact, with Sterne's general delineations of character as it is, I have attempted to show, with his particular passages of sentiment. He is never at his best and truest—as, indeed, no writer of fiction ever is or can be—save when he is allowing his dramatic imagination to play the most freely upon his characters, and thinking least about himself. This is curiously illustrated in his handling of what is, perhaps, the next most successful of the uncaricatured portraits in the Shandy gallery—the presentment of the Rev. Mr. Yorick. Nothing can be more perfect in its way than the picture of the "lively, witty, sensitive, and heedless parson," in chapter x. of the first volume of *Tristram Shandy*. We seem to see the thin, melancholy figure on the rawboned horse—the apparition which could "never present itself in the village but it caught the attention of old and young," so that "labour stood still as he passed, the bucket hung suspended in the middle of the well, the spinning-wheel forgot its round; even chuck-farthing and shuffle-cap themselves stood gaping till he was out of sight." Throughout this chapter Sterne, though describing himself, is projecting his personality to a distance, as it were, and contemplating it dramatically; and the result is excellent. When in the next chapter he becomes "lyrical," so to speak; when the reflection upon his (largely imaginary) wrongs impels him to look inward, the invariable consequence follows; and though Yorick's much bepraised death-scene, with Eugenius at his bed-side, is redeemed from entire failure by an admixture of the humorous with its attempted pathos, we ask ourselves with some wonder what the unhappiness—or the death itself, for that matter—is "all about." The wrongs which were supposed to have broken Yorick's heart are most imperfectly specified (a comic proof, by the way, of Sterne's entire absorption in himself, to the confusion of his own personal knowledge with that of the reader), and the first conditions of enlisting the reader's sympathies are left unfulfilled.

But it is comparatively seldom that this foible of Sterne obtrudes itself upon the strictly narrative and dramatic parts of his work; and, next to the abiding charm and interest of his principal figure, it is by the admirable life and colour of his scenes that he exercises his strongest powers of fascination over a reader. Perpetual as are Sterne's affectations, and tiresome as is his eternal self-consciousness when he is speaking in his own person, yet when once the dramatic instinct fairly lays hold of him there is no writer who ever makes us more completely forget him in the presence of his characters—none who can bring them and their surroundings, their looks and words, before us with such convincing force of reality. One wonders sometimes whether Sterne himself was aware of the high dramatic excellence of many of what actors would call his " carpenter's scenes "—the mere interludes

introduced to amuse us while the stage is being prepared
for one of those more elaborate and deliberate displays of
pathos or humour, which do not always turn out to be
unmixed successes when they come.   Sterne prided himself vastly upon the incident of Le Fevre's death; but I
dare say that there is many a modern reader who would
rather have lost this highly-wrought piece of domestic
drama, than that other exquisite little scene in the kitchen
of the inn, when Corporal Trim toasts the bread which the
sick lieutenant's son is preparing for his father's posset, while
" Mr. Yorick's curate was smoking a pipe by the fire, but
said not a word, good or bad, to comfort the youth."   The
whole scene is absolute life; and the dialogue between the
Corporal and the parson, as related by the former to his
master, with Captain Shandy's comments thereon, is almost
Shakspearian in its excellence.   Says the Corporal:

"When the lieutenant had taken his glass of sack and toast he
felt himself a little revived, and sent down into the kitchen to let me
know that in about ten minutes he should be glad if I would step
upstairs.   I believe, said the landlord, he is going to say his prayers, for there was a book laid on the chair by the bed-side, and as I
shut the door I saw him take up a cushion.   I thought, said the curate, that you gentlemen of the army, Mr. Trim, never said your prayers at all.   I heard the poor gentleman say his prayers last night,
said the landlady, very devoutly, and with my own ears, or I could
not have believed it.   Are you sure of it? replied the curate.   A
soldier, an' please your reverence, said I, prays as often (of his own
accord) as a parson; and when he is fighting for his king, and for
his own life, and for his honour too, he has the most reason to pray
to God of any one in the whole world.   'Twas well said of thee, Trim,
said my Uncle Toby.   But when a soldier, said I, an' please your reverence, has been standing for twelve hours together in the trenches,
up to his knees in cold water—or engaged, said I, for months together in long and dangerous marches; harassed, perhaps, in his rear to-
day; harassing others to-morrow; detached here; countermanded

there; resting this night out upon his arms; beat up in his shirt the next; benumbed in his joints; perhaps without straw in his tent to kneel on, [he] must say his prayers how and when he can. I believe, said I—for I was piqued, quoth the Corporal, for the reputation of the army—I believe, an't please your reverence, said I, that when a soldier gets time to pray, he prays as heartily as a parson—though not with all his fuss and hypocrisy. Thou shouldst not have said that, Trim, said my Uncle Toby; for God only knows who is a hypocrite and who is not. At the great and general review of us all, corporal, at the day of judgment (and not till then) it will be seen who have done their duties in this world and who have not, and we shall be advanced, Trim, accordingly. I hope we shall, said Trim. It is in the Scripture, said my Uncle Toby, and I will show it thee in the morning. In the meantime, we may depend upon it, Trim, for our comfort, said my Uncle Toby, that God Almighty is so good and just a governor of the world, that if we have but done our duties in it, it will never be inquired into whether we have done them in a red coat or a black one. I hope not, said the Corporal. But go on, said my Uncle Toby, with thy story."

We might almost fancy ourselves listening to that noble prose colloquy between the disguised king and his soldiers on the night before Agincourt, in *Henry V*. And though Sterne does not, of course, often reach this level of dramatic dignity, there are passages in abundance in which his dialogue assumes, through sheer force of individualized character, if not all the dignity, at any rate all the impressive force and simplicity, of the "grand style."

Taken altogether, however, his place in English letters is hard to fix, and his tenure in human memory hard to determine. Hitherto he has held his own, with the great writers of his era, but it has been in virtue, as I have attempted to show, of a contribution to the literary possessions of mankind which is as uniquely limited in amount as it is exceptionally perfect in quality. One cannot but feel that, as regards the sum of his titles to recollection, his

name stands far below either of those other two which
in the course of the last century added themselves to
the highest rank among the classics of English humour.
Sterne has not the abounding life and the varied human
interest of Fielding; and, to say nothing of his vast intellectual inferiority to Swift, he never so much as approaches those problems of everlasting concernment to man which
Swift handles with so terrible a fascination. Certainly no
enthusiastic Gibbon of the future is ever likely to say of
Sterne's "pictures of human manners" that they will out-
live the palace of the Escurial and the Imperial Eagle of
the House of Austria. Assuredly no one will ever find in
this so-called English antitype of the Curé of Meudon
any of the deeper qualities of that gloomy and commanding spirit which has been finely compared to the "soul of
Rabelais *habitans in sicco*." Nay, to descend even to minor aptitudes, Sterne cannot tell a story as Swift and Fielding can tell one; and his work is not assured of life as
Tom Jones and *Gulliver's Travels*, considered as stories
alone, would be assured of it, even if the one were strip-
ped of its cheerful humour, and the other disarmed of its
savage allegory. And hence it might be rash to predict
that Sterne's days will be as long in the land of literary
memory as the two great writers aforesaid. Ranked, as
he still is, among "English classics," he undergoes, I suspect, even more than an English classic's ordinary share
of reverential neglect. Among those who talk about him
he has, I should imagine, fewer readers than Fielding, and
very much fewer than Swift. Nor is he likely to increase
their number as time goes on, but rather, perhaps, the contrary. Indeed, the only question is whether with the lapse
of years he will not, like other writers as famous in their
day, become yet more of a mere name. For there is still,

of course, a further stage to which he may decline. That
object of so much empty mouth-honour, the English classic of the last and earlier centuries, presents himself for
classification under three distinct categories.   There is the
class who are still read in a certain measure, though in a
much smaller measure than is pretended, by the great body
of ordinarily well-educated men.   Of this class, the two
authors whose names I have already cited, Swift and Fielding, are typical examples; and it may be taken to include
Goldsmith also.   Then comes the class of those whom the
ordinarily well-educated public, whatever they may pretend,
read really very little or not at all; and in this class we
may couple Sterne with Addison, with Smollett, and, except, of course, as to *Robinson Crusoe*—unless, indeed, our
blasé boys have outgrown him among other pleasures of
boyhood—with Defoe.   But below this there is yet a third
class of writers, who are not only read by none but the
critic, the connoisseur, or the historian of literature, but
are scarcely read even by them, except from curiosity, or
" in the way of business."   The type of this class is Richardson ; and one cannot, I say, help asking whether he will
hereafter have Sterne as a companion of his dusty solitude.
Are *Tristram Shandy* and the *Sentimental Journey* destined to descend from the second class into the third—
from the region of partial into that of total neglect, and to
have their portion with *Clarissa Harlowe* and *Sir Charles
Grandison?* The unbounded vogue which they enjoyed
in their time will not save them ; for sane and sober critics
compared Richardson in his day to Shakspeare, and Diderot broke forth into prophetic rhapsodies upon the immortality of his works which to us in these days have become
absolutely pathetic in their felicity of falsified prediction.
Seeing, too, that a good three-fourths of the attractions

which won Sterne his contemporary popularity are now so
much dead weight of dead matter, and that the vital re-
siduum is in amount so small, the fate of Richardson might
seem to be but too close behind him. Yet it is difficult to
believe that this fate will ever quite overtake him. His
sentiment may have mostly ceased—it probably has ceased
—to stir any emotion at all in these days; but there is an
imperishable element in his humour. And though the
circle of his readers may have no tendency to increase, one
can hardly suppose that a charm, which those who still
feel it feel so keenly, will ever entirely cease to captivate;
or that time can have any power over a perfume which so
wonderfully retains the pungent freshness of its fragrance
after the lapse of a hundred years.

THE END.

THE BROWNING LETTERS

THE LETTERS OF ROBERT BROWNING AND
ELIZABETH BARRETT BARRETT, 1845–1846.
Illustrated with Two Contemporary Portraits of the
Writers, and Two Facsimile Letters. With a Pref-
atory Note by R. BARRETT BROWNING, and Notes,
by F. G. KENYON, Explanatory of the Greek Words.
Two Volumes. Crown 8vo, Cloth, Ornamental, Deckel
Edges and Gilt Tops, $5 00 ; Half Morocco, $9 50.

Many good gifts have come to English literature from the
two Brownings, husband and wife, besides those poems, which
are their greatest. The gift of one's poems is the gift of one's
self. But in a fuller sense have this unique pair now given
themselves by what we can but call the gracious gift of these
letters. As their union was unique, so is this correspondence unique. . . . The letters are the most opulent in various interest which have been published for many a day.—
Academy, London.

We have read these letters with great care, with grow-
ing astonishment, with immense respect ; and the final result
produced on our minds is that these volumes contain one of
the most precious contributions to literary history which our
time has seen.—*Saturday Review*, London.

We venture to think that no such remarkable and unbroken series of intimate letters between two remarkable
people has ever been given to the world. . . . There is
something extraordinarily touching in the gradual unfolding
of the romance in which two poets play the parts of hero
and heroine.—*Spectator*, London.

HARPER & BROTHERS, PUBLISHERS
NEW YORK AND LONDON

☞ *The above work will be sent by mail, postage prepaid, to any part of the United States, Canada, or Mexico,
on receipt of the price.*

BISMARCK'S AUTOBIOGRAPHY

BISMARCK, The Man and the Statesman: Being the
Reflections and Reminiscences of Otto, Prince von
Bismarck, Written and Dictated by Himself after his
Retirement from Office. Translated from the German
under the Supervision of A. J. Butler, late Fellow of
Trinity College, Cambridge. Two Vols. With Two
Photogravure Portraits. 8vo, Cloth, Ornamental, Un-
cut Edges and Gilt Tops, $7 50.

In his reflections and reminiscences, Prince Bismarck presents himself in the more familiar garb of polite society, with
the polished manner of a man of the world, keeping his
tongue under control, a great and commanding figure, self-
centred and self-restrained, a courtier and a statesman, filling
not unworthily with his gigantic personality the world-stage
on which he moved.—*London Times.*

The book is remarkably full as regards internal affairs, and
especially as regards the influences which prevailed at the
Berlin court, as to the characters both of the kings of Prussia
and the other men with whom Bismarck was brought in contact, and it contains a minute criticism on the workings of the
Prussian and German Constitutions.—*London Daily Chronicle.*

This is a great work, one of the most important produced
in modern times. It is a work gloriously full of great lights,
and carries the study of the founding and founded empire
and its inner motives on through the *Culturkampf* down to
the last days of the lamented Frederick I.—*Independent,* N. Y.

HARPER & BROTHERS, Publishers
NEW YORK AND LONDON

☞ *The above work will be sent by mail, postage prepaid,
to any part of the United States, Canada, or Mexico, on receipt of the price.*

By GEORGE WILLIAM CURTIS

By HENRY LAUREN CLINTON

CELEBRATED TRIALS. With Nine Portraits. Crown
  8vo, Cloth, Uncut Edges and Gilt Top, $2 50.

The author has left no need to write up his subject. He
marshals the preliminary facts in each case clearly and dispassionately, and then lets the story in a great measure tell
itself. The author has relied to a considerable extent upon
extracts from the newspapers of the day, to which his own
matter supplies the links as well as a running commentary.
The effect of this method is that his pictures have the old-
time coloring and atmosphere, and we see the events, as it
were, in their proper perspective.—*San Francisco Bulletin.*

The stories will be read for their own absorbing interest,
as well as for the light they throw on municipal history. . . .
We are given facts untouched by fancy, and the stories are
interesting enough in themselves to hold the attention from
beginning to end.—*Saturday Evening Gazette,* Boston.

EXTRAORDINARY CASES. With Photogravure
  Portrait. Crown 8vo, Cloth, Uncut Edges and Gilt
  Top, $2 50.

The number and importance of the cases in which Mr.
Clinton was interested are indeed extraordinary, and their description has for even the unprofessional reader a fascinating
interest. . . . Mr. Clinton's book is interspersed with interesting anecdotes of bench and bar, and cannot fail to interest
lawyer and layman alike.—*N. Y. Mail and Express.*

HARPER & BROTHERS, PUBLISHERS

NEW YORK AND LONDON

☞*Either of the above works will be sent by mail, postage
prepaid, to any part of the United States, Canada, or Mexico,
on receipt of the price.*

THE HAWORTH BRONTË.

WITH BIOGRAPHICAL INTRODUCTIONS

By Mrs. HUMPHRY WARD

This new and uniform edition of the Life and Works of the Brontë Sisters for the first time presents these works in an adequate form. The edition is in seven volumes, viz.:

JANE EYRE.	SHIRLEY.
VILLETTE.	WILDFELL HALL.
WUTHERING HEIGHTS.	THE PROFESSOR.

LIFE OF CHARLOTTE BRONTË. By Mrs. GASKELL. Notes by CLEMENT K. SHORTER.

Illustrated with Photogravures. Bound in Green and Gold, Uncut Edges and Gilt Tops, $1 75 per Volume. Seven Vols., in Box, $12 25.

HARPER & BROTHERS, Publishers
NEW YORK AND LONDON

☞ *Any of the above works will be sent by mail, postage prepaid, to any part of the United States, Canada, or Mexico, on receipt of the price.*

By CHARLES DUDLEY WARNER

THAT FORTUNE. Post 8vo, Half Leather, $1 50.

"That Fortune" is a vivid and powerful portrayal of New York life. It is the third in a trilogy, being in a way a sequel to "A Little Journey in the World" and "The Golden House."

THE PEOPLE FOR WHOM SHAKESPEARE WROTE. 16mo, Cloth, Ornamental, Deckel Edges and Gilt Top, $1 25.

THE RELATION OF LITERATURE TO LIFE. Post 8vo, Cloth, Ornamental, Uncut Edges and Gilt Top, $1 50. (In "Harper's Contemporary Essayists.")

THE GOLDEN HOUSE. Illustrated by W. T. SMEDLEY. Post 8vo, Ornamental Half Leather, Uncut Edges and Gilt Top, $2 00.

A LITTLE JOURNEY IN THE WORLD. A Novel. Post 8vo, Half Leather, Uncut Edges and Gilt Top, $1 50; Paper, 75 cents.

THEIR PILGRIMAGE. Illustrated by C. S. REINHART. Post 8vo, Half Leather, Uncut Edges and Gilt Top, $2 00.

STUDIES IN THE SOUTH AND WEST, with Comments on Canada. Post 8vo, Half Leather, Uncut Edges and Gilt Top, $1 75.

AS WE GO. With Portrait and Illustrations. 16mo, Cloth, Ornamental, $1 00. (In "Harper's American Essayists.")

AS WE WERE SAYING. With Portrait and Illustrations. 16mo, Cloth, Ornamental, $1 00. (In "Harper's American Essayists.")

THE WORK OF WASHINGTON IRVING. With Portraits. 32mo, Cloth, Ornamental, 50 cents. (In Black and White Series.)

Mr. Warner has such a fine fancy, such a genial humor, that one never tires of him.—*Cincinnati Commercial Gazette.*

HARPER & BROTHERS, PUBLISHERS
NEW YORK AND LONDON

☞ *Any of the above works will be sent by mail, postage prepaid, to any part of the United States, Canada, or Mexico, on receipt of the price.*

W. M. THACKERAY'S COMPLETE WORKS

BIOGRAPHICAL EDITION

This New and Revised Edition Comprises Additional Material and Hitherto Unpublished Letters, Sketches, and Drawings, Derived from the Author's Original Manuscripts and Note-books.

Edited by Mrs. ANNE THACKERAY RITCHIE.

1. VANITY FAIR.
2. PENDENNIS.
3. YELLOWPLUSH PAPERS, Etc.
4. BARRY LYNDON, Etc.
5. SKETCH BOOKS, Etc.
6. CONTRIBUTIONS TO "PUNCH."
7. ESMOND, Etc.
8. THE NEWCOMES.
9. CHRISTMAS BOOKS, Etc.
10. THE VIRGINIANS.
11. PHILIP, Etc.
12. DENIS DUVAL, Etc.
13. MISCELLANIES, Etc.

Crown 8vo, Cloth, Uncut Edges and Gilt Tops, $1 75 per Volume.

The edition is one which appeals peculiarly to all Thackeray lovers.—*Philadelphia Ledger.*

Although we are not to have an authorized life of Thackeray, we are to have the next best thing, in the notes that his daughter, Mrs. Richmond Ritchie, has supplied to the biographical edition of her father's work.—*Chicago Tribune.*

The biographical introductions, which promise no little *personalia* fresh to most readers or not before collected, will together invest this edition with unique interest and give it a value which will easily place it at the head of editions of the great English novelist.—*Literary World*, Boston.

HARPER & BROTHERS, PUBLISHERS
NEW YORK AND LONDON